Manager's Guide to
Lean and Performance

Revision 2

Eric M. Gatmaitan

Manager's Guide to Lean and Performance

About the Author

Eric M. Gatmaitan earned a master in business administration degree with an emphasis on business information systems from Western Michigan University and a bachelor of science degree in industrial management engineering with a minor in mechanical engineering from De La Salle University.

Mr. Gatmaitan is the author of the books *Manager's Guide to Lean and Performance*, *Lean and Performance Driven*, and *Beginner's Guide to Crystal Reports© 2013*. He was a faculty member at Western Michigan University, where he taught computer technology application and programming.

In the construction and manufacturing industries, he served as an industrial engineer, production supervisor, plant manager, and chief operating officer.

As a consultant, Mr. Gatmaitan leads projects and conducts training in the areas of strategic planning, business-process optimization, quality systems, and performance management systems.

Copyright © 2015 Eric M. Gatmaitan. All rights reserved. Rev 2

ISBN: 1490406654
ISBN-13: 978-1490406657

© Copyright 2015 Microsoft Corporation. All rights reserved. Used with permission from Microsoft. This book is an independent publication and is not affiliated with, nor has it been authorized, sponsored, or otherwise approved by Microsoft Corporation. Microsoft© Vision, Microsoft© Excel, and Microsoft© Project are registered trademarks of Microsoft Corporation in the United States and other countries.

© Copyright 2015. SAP AG. All rights reserved. This publication contains references to the products of SAP, SAP Business Objects, and other SAP products and services mentioned herein as well as their respective logos and trademarks or registered trademarks of SAP AG in Germany and other countries. Crystal Reports and logos are trademarks or registered trademarks of Business Objects Software Ltd. Business Objects is an SAP company.

Basics of Workplace Organization™ is a trademark of Eric M. Gatmaitan. All rights reserved.
Ant Illustration: Paul Sizer, Sizer Design + Illustration More info at www.paulsizer.com

Table of Contents

Introduction 1

Chapter 1: The Strategic Rationale 15
    Strategy Development 16
    Definition of Terms 17
    Strategic Planning Process 17

Chapter 2: Business-Process Mapping 29
    Elements of a Business-Process Map 30
    Process-Flow Diagram Symbols 33
    Process-Mapping Procedure 36

Chapter 3: Cascading Performance Metrics 41
    Aligning Metrics 41
    Cascading Strategic Metrics 42

Chapter 4: Access to Performance Data 49
    Limitations to Accessing Data 49
    Data Access and Report Development 50

Chapter 5: Project Planning and Management 55
    Project-Planning Process 56
    Project Summary Report 62
    Projects Dashboard 63

Chapter 6: Kaizen Events 65
Process Overview 65
Event Preparation 67
Rules of the Game 68
Implementation Procedure 69

Chapter 7: Corrective-Action Process 77
Process Overview 77
The Nonconformance and Corrective-Action Process
.... 78

Chapter 8: Applying Kanban 87
Managing Inventory and Flow 87
Role of Kanban 89
Advanced-Card-System Design 97

Chapter 9: Bottom-up Performance Reviews 103
Process Overview 103
Technical Support Staff 105
Department Manager as System Administrator 108

Chapter 10: Developing Self-Sufficiency 117
Manage Operations through Work Teams 117
The Supervisor Providing Technical Support 118
Process Compliance 119
A Common Goal Builds Teamwork 120
The Common Goal 121
Providing Performance Feedback 123

Table of Contents

Delegating Team Leadership 124
Routine Performance Review..................................126
Step-by-Step Procedures 129
   Creating the Team Structure...............................130
   Identifying Performance Measures 131
   Collecting Performance Data 132
   Setting Up the Meeting Area...............................133
   Displaying Performance Data 134
   Setting Performance Goals.................................136
   Developing the Meeting Agenda.........................138
   Conducting a Team Meeting...............................139

Chapter 11: Building the Support Structure 141
   The Technical-Support Staff....................................141
   Performance Measures 143
   Presenting Performance Data 143
   The Support-Staff Meeting 144
   Step-by-Step Procedures 147
      Creating the Support-Staff Structure...................148
      Identifying Performance Measures 149
      Presenting Performance Measures 151
      Setting Goals 152
      Establishing the Meeting Area 154
      Developing the Meeting Agenda.........................155
      Conducting a Support-Staff Meeting...................156

Chapter 12: Focus on Compliance 159
   People 161
      Improving Training Compliance 162
      Training Matrix 163
   Machines 164
   Materials 166
   Methods 167
   Data 169
   Step-by-Step Procedures 171
      Creating a Training System 172
      Writing a Work Instruction 173
      Routing a Procedure for Approval...................... 175
      Training Procedure 176
      Improving Procedure Compliance...................... 177
      Revising a Procedure... 178

Chapter 13: Managing Improvements....................... 179
   Constant Focus on Compliance 179
      Performance Data... 179
      Issue-Resolution Scorecard 180
   Employee Suggestion System............................... 181
      Setting Up the Rules of the Game 181
      Implementation 182
      Recognition and Reward..................................... 183
   Step-by-Step Procedures 185
      Tracking Resolution of Issues............................. 186
      Submitting a Suggestion for Improvement.......... 188

Table of Contents

Routing a Suggestion to the Support Staff..........190

Chapter 14: Workplace Organization........................191
   The Five Basics of Workplace Organization...........192
   Implementation 194
   Manufacturing Five Basics Audit Checklist.............196
   Office Five Basics Audit Checklist 198
   Step-by-Step Procedures 201
      Assigning Areas of Responsibility 202
      Conducting the Five Basics Survey 203

Chapter 15: Effective Job Performance Reviews 205
   Design Considerations 205
   Rating System 206
      Change Required 206
      Contributing...207
      Expected 207
      Commendable..207
      Exceptional 208
   Components of a Job-Performance Review...........208
   Performance Measures 209
      Example Performance Measures........................211
   Performance Standards...213
   Rating Sheet..213
      Example JPR Rating Sheet 214
      Example Performance Summary 215
   Completing a JPR Form 216

Review Process 216
Linking JPR to Compensation 217
Implementation 218
Example Implementation Timetable 218
Step-by-Step Procedures 219
    JPR Implementation 220
    JPR System Overview 221
    Completing a JPR Form 222

Conclusion 223

Introduction

No stories, just the process. A compilation of two books. **Building a Citadel** was written for strategic and tactical-level managers while **Lean and Performance Driven** was developed for tactical-level and operations managers.

Building a Citadel outlines the top-down and bottom-up approach for building the organizational discipline and the precision of deploying performance-driven initiatives.

Lean and Performance Driven is a compilation of implementation procedures at establishing a lean environment and a performance-driven work force.

Building a Citadel: A Strategic Guide to Lean

Lean initiatives across all industries seek the best method for an organization to operate effectively and efficiently. This guide to Lean is intended for supervisors and managers with background knowledge or exposure to operations management, including process-improvement programs such as

Introduction

Kaizen, Total Quality Management system, Toyota production system, and Lean Six Sigma.

As an educator and industrial engineer with decades of experience, I continue to document the processes and lessons learned to optimize an organization's journey toward improved capability to operate faster, better, and easier. This book is a compilation of how to implement process improvements that impact performance throughout the entire organization.

This strategic guide to Lean provides a top-down optimization of the core structures and processes of an organization. Optimizing the structural framework will provide big dividends and resolve most of your company's tactical and operational inefficiencies.

Strategic Cascade
Lean and performance-oriented initiatives are effectively deployed as part of an organizational strategy. Resource coordination, interdepartment interfaces, and priorities are aligned when these

initiatives are communicated as directives for achieving corporate objectives. In chapter 1, the strategic planning process outlines the rationale for launching project initiatives such as Lean. This is a quick-start process to strategic planning so organizations can quickly learn, implement, and gain results. I have used this process with organizations to refocus their efforts and deploy a cohesive plan to achieve operational and financial results.

Total business-enterprise optimization starts with a strategic view of the process and drills down to the tactical and operational levels. An optimal path is defined with non-value-adding activities. In chapter 2, a unique business-enterprise-mapping method I developed is outlined. It is a highly effective and efficient method using a blend of industrial engineering, information systems, and instructional design. When executed properly, an enterprise-wide process map can be completed in less than six weeks as compared to conventional methods, which take months and even years. At a Fortune 500 medical-device-manufacturing company, I guided the executive-management team to develop

Introduction

the order-to-cash process map. It took six weeks to complete the process maps and identify process improvements to quicken the order-to-cash process cycle time.

The top-down approach continues in chapter 3 with the cascade of performance metrics. Performance goals are aligned and laid out for the entire organization. Organizational discipline, focus, and precision are established with the following:

1. Unified strategic plan for success
2. Common goal that cascades throughout the entire organization
3. Standardized business-enterprise process

As a plant manager for a medical-device-manufacturing company, I quickly learned that a common set of performance metrics enabled the organization to function effectively and efficiently as a cohesive team. With a disciplined implementation, it is common to see 30 percent improvements in safety, quality, delivery, and cost.

Organizations today are more process driven and rely heavily on performance data to make decisions. Frequent reviews of performance data validate the incremental steps made in achieving the overall goal of the organization. Chapter 4 provides an overview of Crystal Reports© and presents an option for data access, analysis, and presentation. Working with a health-care provider, we were successful at enabling supervisors and managers to develop health-care analytics to improve patient outcomes and administrative processes.

Deployment

Lean and performance-oriented initiatives require a methodical planning and execution process. Chapter 5 features project-planning fundamentals. The process is generally accepted across all industries, including project-management software applications such as Microsoft Project.

Targeted strikes on specific areas of the organization are required to improve performance metrics. Kaizen events, also known as Kaizen Blitz, are fast-attack programs focused on improving a single area. Chapter 6 describes a performance-driven method that follows the plan-do-check-act (PDCA) process-improvement cycle. The same

Introduction

PDCA discipline enabled a pharmaceutical-manufacturing company to improve its on-time delivery rating from 65 percent to 100 percent within a seven-month time frame.

With methods and standards of performance in place, an organization requires a highly disciplined and data-driven approach to investigating nonconformances and applying a corrective action. Chapter 7 provides the framework for identifying the root causes and effectively implementing improvements to eliminate the occurrence of nonconformances. The process has helped numerous organizations in highly regulated industries, such as automotive, medical, and health care, resolve issues objectively and demonstrate a robust business process.

The balance of maintaining the least amount of inventory and assuring on-time delivery of materials is a constant challenge for all organizations. A Kanban process I developed is discussed in chapter 8. It has been used by numerous companies over the past twenty years. It has been proven effective at reducing inventory levels by at least 35 percent and minimizing stock-outs. It is a complementary tool to enterprise resource planning systems. I developed this process when I was a production supervisor at a medical-device-manufacturing company in which finished-product inventory of more than 150 items averaged forty-five days, and yet back orders were a major issue. With Kanban, we balanced the finished-goods inventory to a seven-day supply and eliminated back orders.

The strategic plan outlines the top-down deployment process. Providing feedback on its performance requires a bottom-up approach. Chapter 9 provides an overview of a structured bottom-up performance-review process.

Organizational discipline requires a focus on process compliance and a method for targeting process improvements. Chapter 10 shows a method for enhancing process compliance and an effective employee suggestion process.

Achieving organizational discipline, focus, and precision starts at the strategic level and requires a tactical infrastructure to swiftly respond to dynamic changes in the market arena and enhance operational readiness. Before deploying Lean at the operational level, make certain that the strategic- and tactical-level infrastructure are optimized.

Lean and Performance Driven

The goal of an operations manager is to deliver goods and services that meet an organization's established performance standards for safety, quality, delivery, and cost. Achieving the performance standards requires a manager to go beyond managing people. It extends to managing *all* resources: people, equipment, materials, methods, and data. The definition of a system—a group of interrelated elements working together toward a common goal—outlines the key components of building a performance-driven organization.

I initially developed the methods in this book during my days as a production supervisor for a medical device company. The successful implementation of these methods elevated me to a managerial position with overall responsibility of an entire division. For more than twenty-five years, as an industrial engineer and management consultant, I continued to use the same methods, further improving and validating their effectiveness at enhancing organizational performance.

This book outlines the fundamental structure necessary to establish and manage an effective workforce. The step-by-step guide found at the end of each chapter is a compilation of processes implemented in various industries, from small mom-and-pop businesses to large Fortune 100 companies. Process-improvement tools used in initiatives such as Lean Six Sigma, Total Quality Management, and the Toyota Production System are most effective, and long lasting, when the fundamental structure listed in this book has been implemented.

In my first supervisory job, for a medical device company, the production team was working ten hours a day Monday through Saturday and half a day on Sunday. Product demand was growing, and the production team built up inventory for thirty-one

Introduction

days, yet back orders were a major customer service issue.

In response, we developed a management support-staff and team structure that focused on key performance measures, including product inventory targets. Within the first four weeks of launching the structured organizational process, the performance data guided the team to small-lot production, balancing production requirements to specific product demands. Production hours were scaled back to regular hours, and work orders were cut by 50 percent. This enabled us to reduce product inventory to a nine-day supply and reduce back orders by 75 percent, significantly improving customer service.

This book illustrates the process used to impact performance measures.

Chapter 10 outlines the structure of and methods for establishing an operational-level team environment. It also provides methods for supervisors to manage day-to-day activities through a team structure.

Long-term viability of a team structure hinges on a support staff that monitors team performance and provides technical assistance. In chapter 11, the bottom-up support structure is presented. This structure allows an organization to gather data on operational performance and swiftly address issues that slow down work teams or stop them from achieving their objectives.

Crucial to the work-team and support-staff structure is an organizational focus on compliance of every resource element throughout the entire supply chain. Chapter 12 examines the requirements of people, machines, materials, methods, and data to achieve total-system compliance.

Maintaining and improving compliance requires vigilance at identifying symptomatic issues that lead to nonconformance and the implementation of incremental improvements.

Chapter 13 presents a simple but robust process of issue resolution and employee suggestion that will enable employees to eliminate issues proactively and participate in continuous improvement efforts. An open and robust implementation of the process

Introduction

detailed in chapter 13 requires a decentralized delegation of responsibility and authority. When the process is implemented properly, you can expect rapid improvements that are fun for the entire organization. I have seen numerous work teams implement two process improvements per person per month, or two hundred process improvements per month in an organization with one hundred people.

Chapter 14 outlines the process for implementing the Five Basics of Workplace Organization, also known as 5S. This chapter includes an audit checklist to help kick off an organizational standard for workplace organization in both office and manufacturing environments. Amazingly, I have seen companies implement the process in chapter 14 effectively and reduce inventory by 35 percent within a month.

An easy-to-use, data-driven, and objective performance-review system provides a closed-loop mechanism to motivate employees to participate fully in a structured and performance-driven work environment. Chapter 15 presents a job-performance-review (JPR) system that is supervisor and employee friendly. During the implementation process, supervisors should maintain focus on the desired operational outcome of the concepts of *lean and performance*. Across all industries, *lean* refers to the efficient use of people, machines, materials, methods, and data. Eliminating waste and streamlining the operation is a constant pursuit. A set of key performance measures balances the outcomes of safety, quality, delivery, and cost. This enables a high-perfomance team to function independently, apply corrective action, and continually improve the process. As a plant manager for a medical device company, I witnessed a fully coordinated workforce with minimal gray areas on objectives and goals. Everyone was data driven, objective, process compliant, and customer focused.

With a structured process and successful implementation, an organization can realize significant productivity gains and improve employee morale.

Introduction

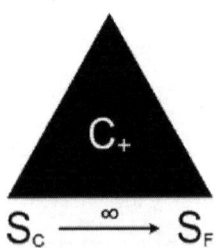

**Infinite Improvements
to the Current State**

© 2013 Eric M. Gatmaitan

Chapter 1: The Strategic Rationale

The rationale for implementing process-improvement initiatives, such as Lean or Total Quality Management, must be tied into the strategic objectives of the organization.

In the development of a corporate strategic plan, programs, projects, and process-improvement initiatives are identified to execute a corporate strategy. A top-down directive communicates a unified plan and the requirements to execute specific project initiatives.

In this chapter, a strategic planning process is outlined; this can be used as a guide in developing a simplified strategic plan. Further research and reading are recommended to improve the level of complexity of a strategic plan.

Strategy Development

The strategic planning process is a widely used planning process with the goal of coordinating company resources to work in harmony at achieving a common objective. The process, also known as corporate planning or CorPlan, requires analyzing current company capabilities, researching market dynamics, understanding the competitive arena, and gathering information on a wider array of factors, such as governmental, societal, and ecological concerns.

The planning process includes identifying market opportunities, threats, and strategies and outlining the course of action necessary for achieving company goals.

The process in this book outlines the major components and processes of developing a strategic plan. Use this process for developing short-, medium-, or even long-term plans. The level of simplicity or complexity of a strategic plan is on a per-user-need basis.

Start with a simple, straightforward strategic plan, and update it every six to twelve months. Gradually increase the level of complexity of the strategic planning process over the years.

Definition of Terms

Objective: Something sought or aimed to achieve.

Strategy: The planned movement to position an organization in a favorable state.

Program: A project or initiative supporting the achievement of a strategy.

Contingency: A potential event that may alter or influence assumptions made in formulating strategies and programs.

Strategic Planning Process

The executive-management team typically initiates the strategic planning process with a series of activities such as compiling data, conducting research, and preparing the base data. Research analysts have to complete steps 1, 3, and 4 before the executive-management team convenes to complete the strategic plan.

Step 1: Analyze the Company Background

Research and compile the data requirements listed below. As much as possible, graph or chart the data.

History

1. What is the story behind the start of the organization?

2. How did the business and product evolve?

3. What are the historical milestones of the organization? Include the high and low points.

4. What is the historical sales performance?

5. Is product mix a major consideration?

6. List other historical financial and/or operational data.

Organization

1. What is the current organizational structure?

2. Is the current organizational structure adequate?

3. Is the organization appropriately staffed with qualified personnel?

4. Are the functional responsibilities defined?

5. Are performance indicators and objectives defined for each functional area?

Mission Statement Analysis

1. What is the current mission statement?

2. What are the intended product and/or service benefits?

3. What are the target markets or industries?

4. Who are the target end-user customers?

5. Is there a need to update the mission statement?

Analysis of Company Activities

1. What are the current product and/or service benefits?

2. What are the best products and/or services?

3. What are the worst products and/or services?

4. What markets and industries are being served?

5. Who are the current end-user customers?

6. Is the business process adequately defined and functioning as intended?

The Strategic Rationale

Resource Assessment

List the current capabilities and limitations of the company using the matrix below.

	Capabilities	Limitations
Conceive and design		
Market		
Manufacture the product		
Provide the service		
Distribute the product		
Provide customer service		
Manage the business process		

Step 2: Identify the Strengths and Limitations

Identify the strengths and limitations as viewed internally (within the organization) and externally (as viewed by customers and competitors).

	Strengths	*Limitations*
Internal		
External		

Step 3: Define the Arena of Competition

Conduct market and competitive analyses to provide the landscape of the competitive arena. The analysis will define the target market profile and its characteristics.

1. What markets are currently being served?

2. What are the target markets?

3. Who are the competitors?

The Strategic Rationale

4. What products are provided to each market?

5. How does the company compete in the market?

6. What services are offered to each market?

7. What are your competitors' advantages?

8. What are your competitors' disadvantages?

Compile the data gathered in the matrix below.

	Market 1	Market 2
The competitors		
Product group		
Method of competition		
Services offered		
Competitor advantage		
Competitor disadvantage		

Step 4: Conduct an Environmental Analysis

Industry Analysis
Conduct an industry analysis outlining the general industry performance, trends, emerging markets, declining markets, industry threats, and opportunities.

Economic Concerns
Identify local, regional, state, or US economic factors that may impact the target markets. Also, include the global economic factors that may impact the target markets.

Governmental Concern
Identify any laws that may impact the target markets.

Technological Environment
Identify new technology that may influence the dynamics of the market, end-users, product quality, cost, and/or manufacturing methods.

Societal & Ecological Concerns
Identify any potential public concerns of product use and its impact to the ecological environment.

Step 5: Identify Market Opportunities and Threats

Examine the competitive market, market research, and environmental analysis. Identify the opportunities and threats for each target market.

	Market 1	Market 2
Opportunities		
Threats		

Step 6: Define the Strategic Objective

Clearly define the objective of the organization for the time period covered by the strategic plan. The objective must identify the performance metric, the current state, the future state, and the completion date. An example of a strategic objective is listed below:

> *Grow sales from $5 million in 2015 to $15 million by 2018 while maintaining net income at 10 percent.*

Step 7: Develop Strategies

Develop strategies to support the achievement of the objective. Strategies are big movements within the organization and the target markets. Examples of strategies are:

1 Penetrate Market 1 and capture 5 percent market share.

2 Expand base account sales in Market 2 by 12 percent.

Step 8: Identify Programs, Projects, and Process-Improvement Initiatives

Identify initiatives and the target implementation dates for each strategy.

1 Penetrate Market 1 and capture 5 percent market share.
  - *New product release Spring 2018*
  - *Manufacturing cost reduction, 10 percent by October 2018*

2 Expand base account sales in Market 2 by 12 percent.
  - *Reduce product price by 5 percent by July 2018*
  - *Release expanded product line offering by 20 percent by May 2018*

Step 9: Develop a Contingency Plan

Identify critical assumptions behind each strategy. Examine assumptions in the market analysis, identification of market threats/opportunities, and the environmental analysis. Answer the questions below to outline the contingency plan.

1. Identify critical issues or events that could possibly hinder the strategy and program implementation.

2. What are the alternate strategies and programs?

3. What are the trigger points to implement the contingency plan?

Step 10: Approve and Release the Strategic Plan

Publish the strategic plan as a formal document for the entire organization to follow and execute. Route the strategic plan for management review and approval.

Step 11: Monitor Compliance and Data Integrity

The strategic plan is intended to be reviewed on a routine basis for changes in market data and plan assumptions. Data is continually compiled in preparation for the next strategic planning session.

The Strategic Rationale

Chapter 2: Business-Process Mapping

The first step in understanding how things work is by documenting the process schematics from start to finish. In a business enterprise, it is the order-to-cash process.

A strategic-cascade approach in business-process mapping is featured in this chapter. It is developed using a blend of the principles of industrial engineering, information systems, and instructional design.

The business-process-mapping activity starts at a strategic level and drills down to the tactical and operational levels. A disciplined approach outlines the optimal path and identifies the less desirable process routines.

The process-flow diagram is complemented by a procedure document. It lists the main steps of the process flow along with key points and identifies process responsibilities.

It is highly recommended that managers document the business-process maps before writing work instructions. Work instructions will complement process maps when detailed step-by-step procedures are necessary. In most cases, high compliance with a business-process map minimizes the need for detailed work instructions.

Elements of a Business-Process Map
The completed business-process map contains (1) a process-flow diagram and (2) a procedure section.

The process-flow diagram shows the sequence of events and how the logical decision should flow. The most efficient path is clearly visible as a straight path flowing down, while the least desirable, and often non-value-adding, activities are shown flowing sideways.

Manager's Guide to Lean and Performance

Example Process-Flow Diagram

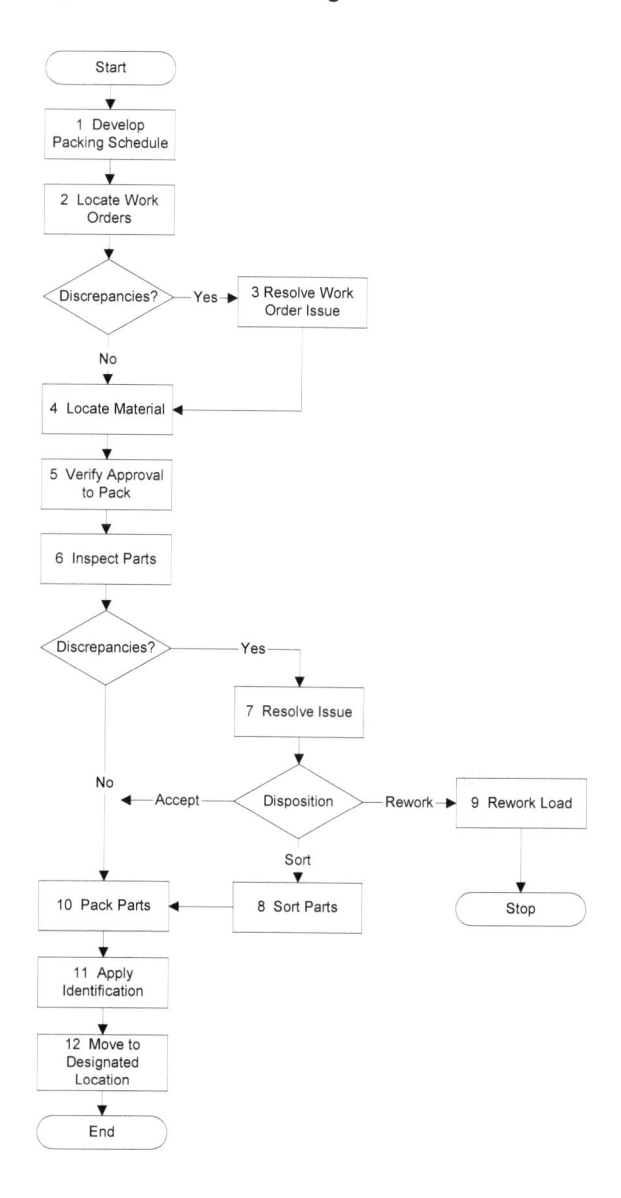

```
Start
  │
  ▼
1 Develop Packing Schedule
  │
  ▼
2 Locate Work Orders
  │
  ▼
Discrepancies? ──Yes──► 3 Resolve Work Order Issue
  │                           │
  No                          │
  ▼                           │
4 Locate Material ◄───────────┘
  │
  ▼
5 Verify Approval to Pack
  │
  ▼
6 Inspect Parts
  │
  ▼
Discrepancies? ──Yes──► 7 Resolve Issue
  │                           │
  No                          ▼
  │                     Disposition ──Rework──► 9 Rework Load
  │                      │      │                     │
  │                   Accept   Sort                   ▼
  │                      │      │                    Stop
  │                      │      ▼
  │                      │   8 Sort Parts
  ▼                      │      │
10 Pack Parts ◄──────────┴──────┘
  │
  ▼
11 Apply Identification
  │
  ▼
12 Move to Designated Location
  │
  ▼
End
```

The procedure section lists the main steps, key points, and who has the responsibility.

Example Procedure Section

Main Step	Key Points	Responsibility
1. Develop Packing Schedule	1.1 Priority list	Line Lead Foreman
2. Locate Work Orders	2.1 Packing desk 2.2 Book	Pack
3. Resolve Work-Order Issue	3.1 Contact supervisor	Pack Line Lead
4. Locate Material	4.1 Unracking/ holding area	Pack
5. Verify Approval to Pack	5.1 Green stamp 5.2 Return to unracking If no green stamp	Pack

Manager's Guide to Lean and Performance

Process-Flow Diagram Symbols

For simplicity, limit the use of flow-charting symbols to the Terminator, Process, Line Connector, Decision, and Connector symbols.

A *Terminator* symbol indicates the starting point and ending point of a process. Terminator symbols include Start, Stop, and End.

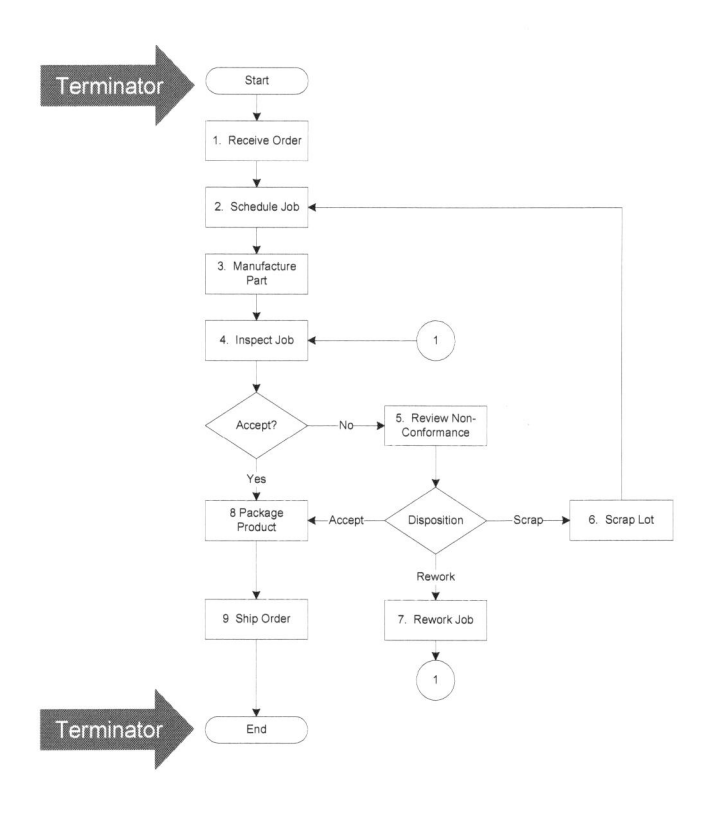

Business - Process Mapping

The *Process* symbol is represented by a rectangle using the format below and describes a main step.

<Action> <Object>

Examples: Schedule Work Order
            Assemble Product
            Prepare Shipment

Keep the main step short and simple. Details will be listed in the procedure document.

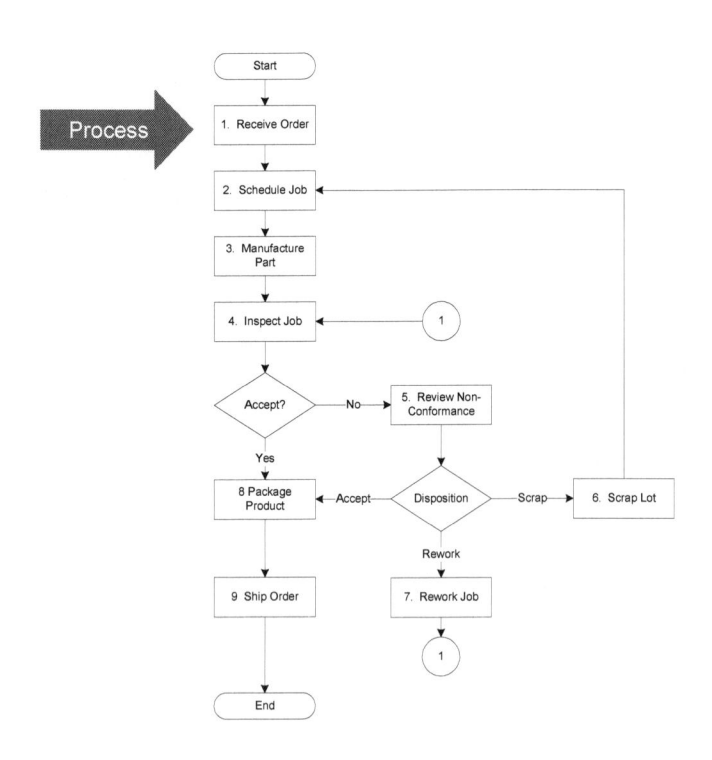

Process →

```
                    Start
                      ↓
            1. Receive Order
                      ↓
            2. Schedule Job ←─────────────┐
                      ↓                   │
            3. Manufacture Part           │
                      ↓                   │
            4. Inspect Job  ←──── (1)     │
                      ↓                   │
                  <Accept?> ──No──→ 5. Review Non-Conformance
                      │                   ↓
                     Yes                  <Disposition>
                      ↓        ←─Accept─      │    ─Scrap─→ 6. Scrap Lot
            8 Package Product               Rework
                      ↓                       ↓
            9 Ship Order                7. Rework Job
                      ↓                       ↓
                    End                      (1)
```

34

Manager's Guide to Lean and Performance

The Line Connector directs the process pathway from one symbol to another. Line connectors are labeled when directing multiple pathway options.

A Decision symbol is a junction where the process is routed based on a decision, result, or output. The preceding Process symbol generates an outcome for the Decision symbol. Line connectors identify the pathway options.

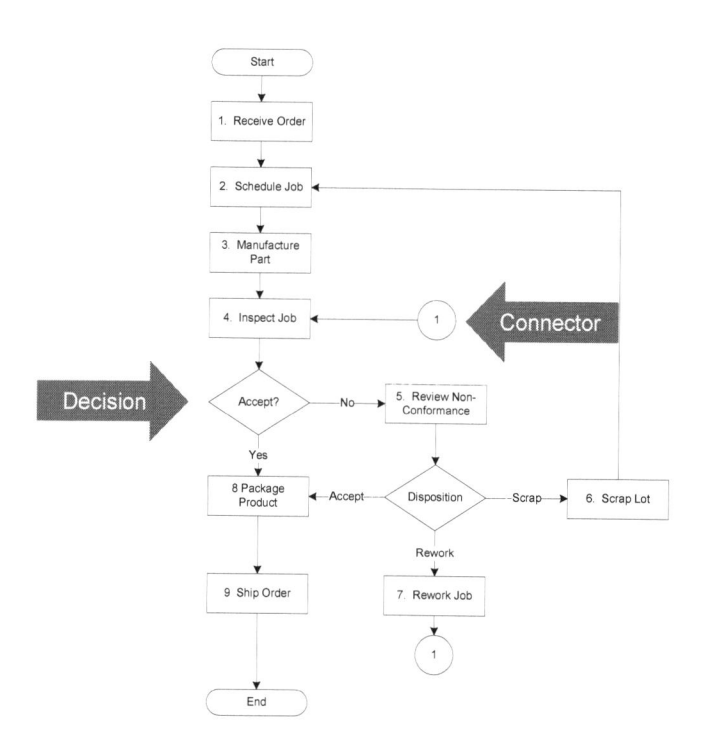

A *Connector* symbol is a utility that maintains simplicity and clarity in the process-flow diagram. Use this to eliminate overlapping line connectors, and link one process to another. Identify each connector numerically.

Process-Mapping Procedure

Step 1: Develop a Process-Flow Diagram

Outline the business process at a very high level or strategic view. List the main steps only. Use a flow-charting software, such as Microsoft Visio, to produce a legible diagram. Here are the process-flow-diagram guidelines:

- Keep the process map simple and easy to understand.
- Use connectors to eliminate overlapping lines.
- Limit the process map to a single page.
- Number each process symbol.
- Develop a straight-line flow indicating the best-case scenario.
- Direct nonideal pathways to the side.

Manager's Guide to Lean and Performance

The Optimal or Ideal Flow

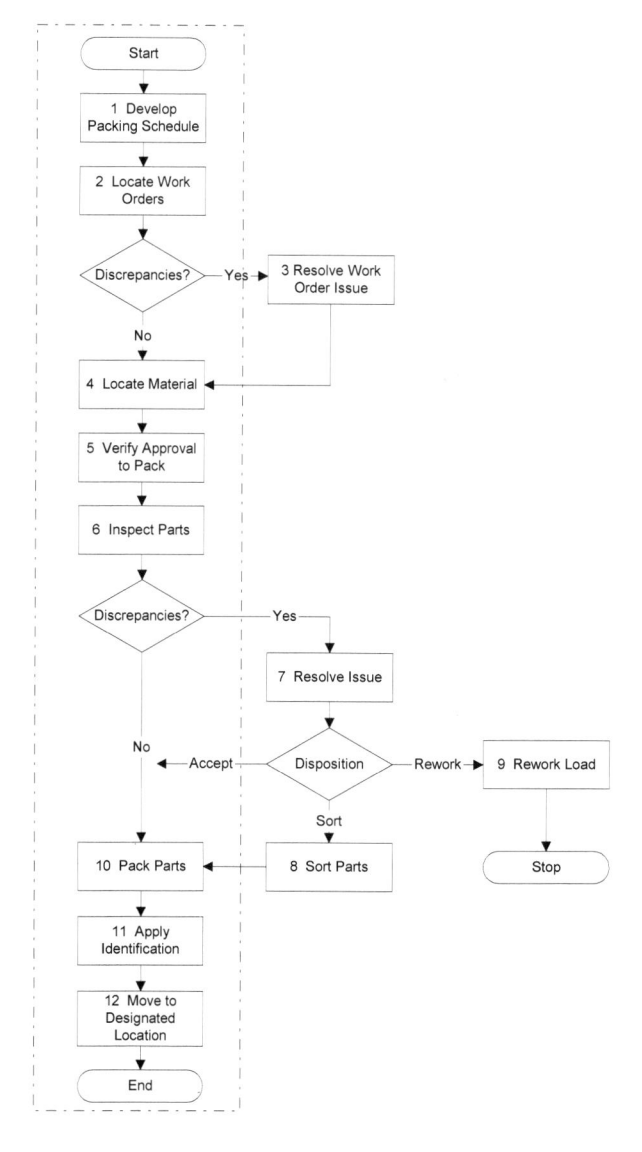

```
Start
  ↓
1 Develop Packing Schedule
  ↓
2 Locate Work Orders
  ↓
Discrepancies? —Yes→ 3 Resolve Work Order Issue
  │ No                        │
  ↓                           │
4 Locate Material ←───────────┘
  ↓
5 Verify Approval to Pack
  ↓
6 Inspect Parts
  ↓
Discrepancies? —Yes→ 7 Resolve Issue
  │ No                        ↓
  │             Accept ← Disposition → Rework → 9 Rework Load
  │                           ↓ Sort                ↓
  ↓                      8 Sort Parts              Stop
10 Pack Parts ←────────────────┘
  ↓
11 Apply Identification
  ↓
12 Move to Designated Location
  ↓
End
```

37

Business - Process Mapping

Resource-extensive and Undesired Processes

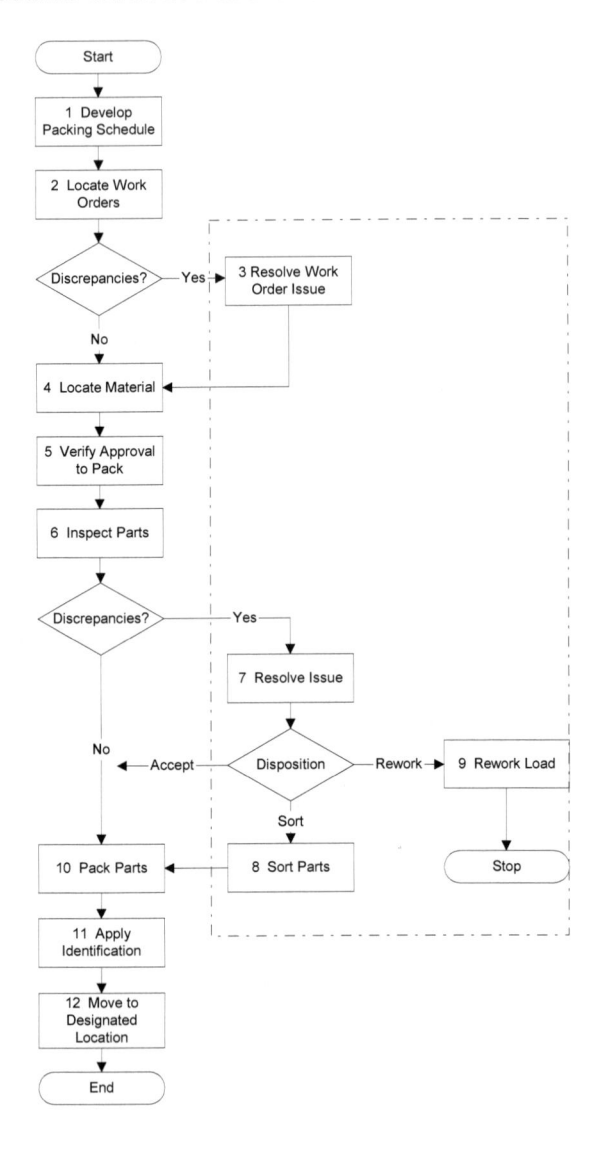

```
Start
  ↓
1 Develop Packing Schedule
  ↓
2 Locate Work Orders
  ↓
Discrepancies? —Yes→ 3 Resolve Work Order Issue
  │ No
  ↓
4 Locate Material
  ↓
5 Verify Approval to Pack
  ↓
6 Inspect Parts
  ↓
Discrepancies? —Yes→ 7 Resolve Issue
  │ No                      ↓
  │              Disposition
  │         Accept / Sort / Rework
  │        ←Accept    ↓Sort    Rework→ 9 Rework Load
  │                8 Sort Parts             ↓
  ↓        ←                              Stop
10 Pack Parts
  ↓
11 Apply Identification
  ↓
12 Move to Designated Location
  ↓
End
```

Step 2: Verify the Accuracy of the Process Map

Enlist the expertise of end-users to validate the accuracy of the process-flow diagram. Monitor the current process, and validate the process-flow diagram.

Step 3: List the Main Steps in the Procedure

Copy the main steps listed in the process-flow diagram, excluding the decision symbol text.

Step 4: List Key Points

Identify a maximum of eight key points for each main step. These key points may include the following:

- Safety precautions
- Assembly specifications
- Verification requirements
- Product handling and care tips
- Documentation requirements

Step 5: Assign Responsibility

Identify the job function or department responsible for executing each main step. Multiple departments may be listed for a specific main step.

Step 6: Route Document for Approval

Apply document control notations as specified by the quality-system procedures, and route the document for approval.

Step 7: Conduct Training

When training on the process map, state the objective and end result. Use the process-flow diagram to explain the logical flow. Reference the procedure section to highlight key points and responsibilities.

Step 8: Develop Tactical-Level Process Maps

Each main step in the strategic-level process map is a potential area for developing a tactical-level process map. About 70 percent of the main steps will require a tactical-level process map.

Step 9: Develop Operational-Level Process Maps

Operational-level process maps are developed on a per-need basis. An estimated 25 percent of tactical-level main steps require an operational-level process map.

Chapter 3: Cascading Performance Metrics

Aligning Metrics

Organizational focus on performance requires a top-down cascade of performance metrics. This is similar to the cascading effect of a strategic plan and the business-process-mapping method explained in chapters 1 and 2.

Performance metrics and diagnostic measures are more meaningful when they are linked throughout the organization. A cascade of performance metrics, a strategic plan, and the business process creates the basis for organizational discipline and purpose. It links every person to a common goal.

Cascading Strategic Metrics

Strategic-Level Metrics

Step 1: Identify the Financial Metrics

The executive-management team reviews the profit-and-loss (P&L) statement and assigns department responsibility to the P&L line items and general ledger accounts.

Step 2: Identify the Strategic Plan Metrics

Examine the programs, projects, and process-improvement initiatives listed in the strategic plan. Identify performance metrics that reflect the execution of initiatives, such as a project summary report. Diagnostics measures may also be used to indicate the effectiveness of a program.

Step 3: Identify Quality Systems, Regulatory Affairs, and Safety Metrics

Incorporate metrics for quality-system management review, regulatory affairs, safety, and other corporate concerns. Limit the review to strategic-level metrics only. The details of nonconformances or audits are delegated to tactical- and operational-level reviews.

Step 4: Define Strategic-Level Metrics and Sources of Data

Create a listing of performance metrics by responsibility. A short definition of the performance metric clarifies the measurement details. Identifying the sources of data assures that all are referencing the same data set. Also, by identifying the data source, the organization will firm up and refine the data-collection process to assure data integrity—timeliness and accuracy.

Step 5: Schedule Routine Strategic-Level Management Review

Set a routine for the executive-management team to review the performance metrics by area of responsibility. Each manager should review the assigned performance metric, highlight variances from the plan, and identify the recommended action plan to correct unfavorable variances. A separate project-review session may be scheduled, if necessary.

Tactical-Level Performance Metrics

Step 6: Assign Department-Level Responsibility

The strategic-level manager meets with the subordinate tactical-level managers to review department-performance measures. Assign responsibility for each performance metric. Multiple tactical-level managers may be assigned to the same performance metric.

Step 7: Identify Tactical-Level Diagnostic Measures

Each tactical-level manager identifies diagnostic measures for the assigned strategic-level performance metric. Diagnostic measures are detailed data sets that align to the attainment of strategic-level performance objectives.

Step 8: Identify Quality Systems, Regulatory Affairs, and Safety Metrics

A detailed examination of compliance and system requirements is conducted at the tactical level. Each nonconformance is reviewed, and each corrective action is monitored to completion.

Diagnostic measures will include items received, items closed, open items, and date of oldest open item.

Step 9: Define the Department-Level Metrics and Sources of Data

Create a listing of performance metrics, sources of data, and responsibility.

Step 10: Schedule Tactical-Level Reviews

Schedule a routine review of tactical-level metrics with all managers, supervisors, and support staff. Every member reviews his or her assigned performance metric, highlights variances from the plan, and identifies the recommended action plan to correct unfavorable variances. The details from this review process prepare the department manager for the strategic-level metrics review.

Operational-Level Performance Metrics

Step 11: Identify Operational-Level Diagnostic Measures for Each Work Team

The tactical-level manager meets with the subordinate operational-level supervisors to review the assigned operational-level performance measures. Assign responsibility for each performance metric and diagnostic measure. Multiple tactical-level managers may be assigned to the same performance metric.

Step 12: Identify Quality Systems, Regulatory Affairs, and Safety Metrics

For the operational team, the primary focus is compliance. The metric will be the number of items received for nonconformances. At the metrics review, the team examines the potential causes of the noncompliance and assists the tactical-level managers in identifying the root cause(s).

Step 13: Define the Work Team Metrics and Sources of Data

Create a listing of performance metrics, sources of data, and responsibilities.

Step 14: Schedule Operational-Level Reviews

In general, work teams review performance data on a daily basis. The performance review is limited to fifteen minutes and follows a strict meeting agenda.

Cascading Performance Metrics

Chapter 4: Access to Performance Data

Limitations to Accessing Data

Organizations are often restricted in their selection of performance metrics and diagnostic measures due to limited capabilities at extracting data. Typically, organizations rely on enterprise resource planning (ERP) system standard reports, and managers realize that they are limited. Managers quickly learn the process of downloading ERP data into a spreadsheet and then performing their data analysis and reporting offline.

Strategic- and tactical-level managers are expected to be experts in data analysis and presentation. They are proficient at using spreadsheets and presentation software. Unfortunately, access to ERP data is often limited.

Front-End Application and Back-End Database

ERP, MRP, and accounting systems are developed in two segments. The front-end application contains the programming codes, and the back-end database contains the data tables and view tables. A view table.

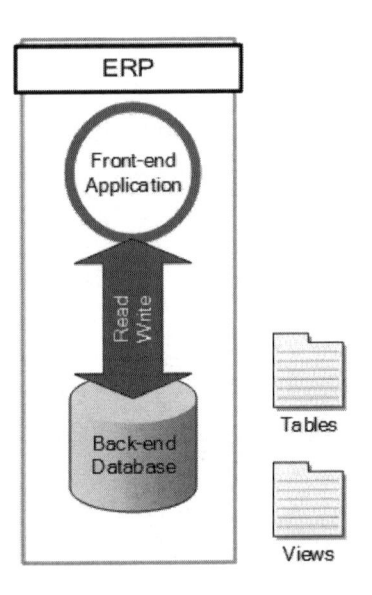

Data Access and Report Development

Crystal Reports©, a product of SAP Business Objects, is a report writer that reads data from virtually any data source. It is the gold standard for report writing. Developers of ERP systems and accounting systems embed Crystal Reports© as part of their software.

Users can create reports containing raw data, summaries of performance metrics, and charts and graphs. Summary reports may also include drill-down options to list detailed data.

Having the option to access multiple data sources enables a user to merge data from an ERP system, production system, accounting system, and even a stand-alone spreadsheet. This feature opens up numerous options for data collection and reporting.

Most people perceive Crystal Reports© as an application restricted for use by IT departments and programmers. Managers who are proficient in using spreadsheets will be able to learn Crystal Reports© with ease. Those with knowledge in programming can learn it very quickly. Managers should consider learning Crystal Reports© as a tool for data analysis.

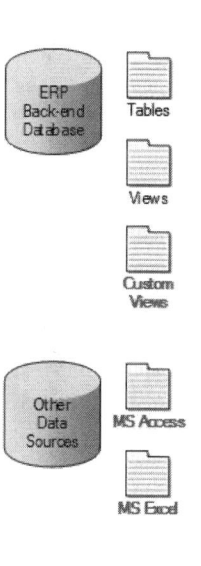

Here is an example report with summary data and a chart embedded:

Access to Performance Data

Here is an example report with summary data and a chart embedded.

On-Time Delivery % : Top 20 Items   Date Range: 01-Jan to 31-Jul

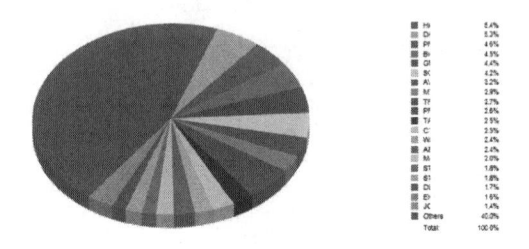

Top 20	Total X-10 1	Total Units	On-Time %	Ontime : Total
uito೦೦	929,662	1,704,850	87.05	1,039 / 1,193
aXлаьа	875,304	1,651,820	96.62	1,660 / 1,718
ಎಂಣಿಂಧಂ೫	750,581	1,437,921	86.31	1,160 / 1,344
puiಗಿರಣಿX೦ಂ	884,944	1,466,760	69.07	862 / 1,248
ಓಎಂಪಾಂದಿಗಿಗಿಆ	552,242	1,378,535	86.68	1,282 / 1,479
ಎಂ⅄೩೦ dd๒	335,927	1,324,376	69.11	3,804 / 5,504
⅄ಎ⅄⅄ಎಎ	502,564	1,003,528	67.48	503 / 575
ಆಔಎ	440,463	910,417	98.96	668 / 675
ಉಎಎ೦	323,596	651,672	31.46	17 / 54
ಎ೦ಎಎಂ	285,492	811,667	84.62	242 / 286
ಜ‌⅄ಎ-೦೦	334,761	794,569	96.27	774 / 804
ಆ೦y	399,253	782,430	87.79	575 / 655
ಐ⅄Oಎ⅄ಎ ಎಎ⅄	448,175	751,107	100.00	1,522 / 1,522
⅄Oಎ	343,961	735,462	63.09	282 / 447
aXಇಎಂಆ	254,409	614,024	80.70	138 / 171
ಆೆಆಎ⅄ಎXಎಎ	150,889	561,402	98.19	541 / 551
ಎಎಎಎ	1,759,941	561,145	80.04	1,500 / 1,874
ಎಎಂX	241,515	547,418	64.37	318 / 494
ಎಂಎಂಊಖ‌ಎಉಆ	172,714	500,175	64.19	213 / 255
ಎಂಎXಇ	172,026	446,927	75.76	100 / 132
ೊ · ೊ, ⌣ ⋯	10,965,961	12,513,245	74.58	12,096 / 16,098
Report Summary	**20,738,469**	**31,289,653**		

Overall On-Time %	% Early > 5 Days	% Early 2-5 Days	% On-Time 0-2 Days Early	% Late 1-2 Days	% Late 2-5 Days	% Late > 5 Days
77.89	19.59	17.11	41.19	7.20	5.93	8.97

IT support may be required to perform the initial setup of the data connection, such as the ODBC connection. After a PC or user terminal is set up with the data connection, the manager can freely develop reports without fear of compromising system data. Crystal Reports© is a read-only data application; it does not have the utility to overwrite data.

Performance metrics and diagnostic measures can also be presented in a dashboard format showing live data with automatic updating on a timed interval.

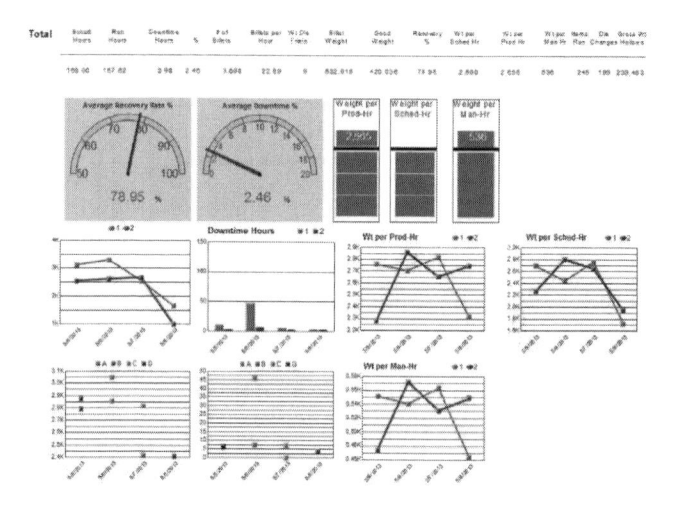

Just like using a spreadsheet, the more hands-on practice managers get, the higher the proficiency in using the application

Access to Performance Data

Chapter 5: Project Planning and Management

The fundamentals of project planning and management have remained consistent over the past decades. The complexity and range of options to be included in a project plan are user dependent. This chapter walks through the fundamental process for planning and managing projects. It is consistent with the knowledge required to use popular project-management software such as Microsoft Project.

Definition of Terms

Milestones: A list of major steps or phases to complete a project.

Tasks: Detailed activities required to complete a project milestone.

Predecessor: The identification of a prerequisite task or milestone. A task with an identified predecessor can start only when the predecessor task is marked 100 percent complete.

Critical Path: A set of milestones and tasks that affect the overall due date of the project. Completing a task ahead of time can provide more time for other tasks, while a delay on a single task in the critical path will delay the entire project.

Project-Planning Process

Step 1: Define the Objective, Scope, and Completion Date

Select a project name, objective, and scope. For projects that interface to the business process, the scope will include the start of the project process, the interface to the current business process, and the end of the project process.

Step 2: Identify the Team Members

Identify the project leader and the core project members. It is best to limit membership in the core project team to four to six people. All others are identified as a resource for implementation.

Step 3: Outline the Project Milestones

Create an outline listing the major steps or phases of the project. Detailed tasks will be listed later.

Example: Project Milestone

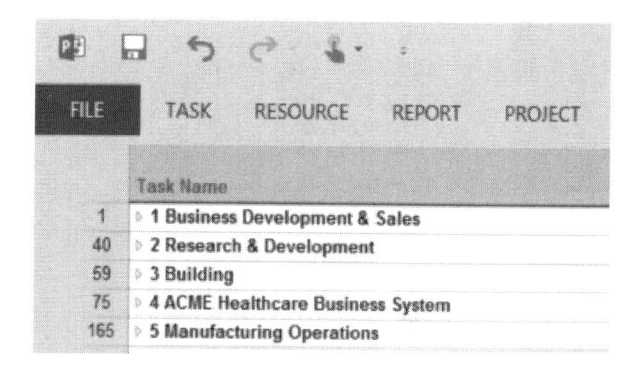

	Task Name
1	▷ 1 Business Development & Sales
40	▷ 2 Research & Development
59	▷ 3 Building
75	▷ 4 ACME Healthcare Business System
165	▷ 5 Manufacturing Operations

Step 4: Identify Tasks for Each Milestone

List the tasks associated to each milestone. These are detailed activities required to complete a project milestone. Identify subtasks, if necessary, to expand detail level.

Project Planning and Management

Example: Tasks and Subtasks

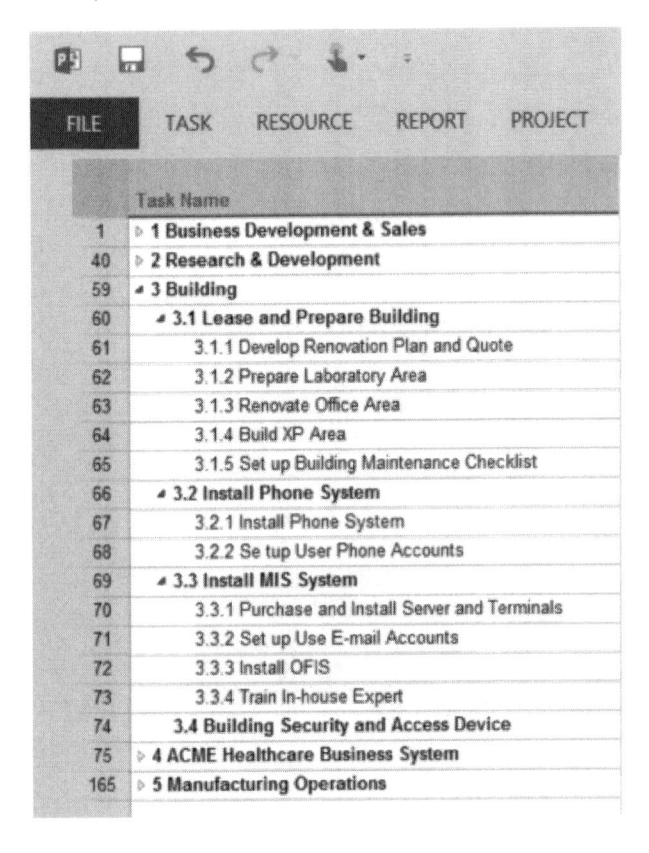

	Task Name
1	▷ 1 Business Development & Sales
40	▷ 2 Research & Development
59	▲ 3 Building
60	▲ 3.1 Lease and Prepare Building
61	3.1.1 Develop Renovation Plan and Quote
62	3.1.2 Prepare Laboratory Area
63	3.1.3 Renovate Office Area
64	3.1.4 Build XP Area
65	3.1.5 Set up Building Maintenance Checklist
66	▲ 3.2 Install Phone System
67	3.2.1 Install Phone System
68	3.2.2 Se tup User Phone Accounts
69	▲ 3.3 Install MIS System
70	3.3.1 Purchase and Install Server and Terminals
71	3.3.2 Set up Use E-mail Accounts
72	3.3.3 Install OFIS
73	3.3.4 Train In-house Expert
74	3.4 Building Security and Access Device
75	▷ 4 ACME Healthcare Business System
165	▷ 5 Manufacturing Operations

Step 5: Determine the Estimated Task Duration

Review each task, and provide an estimated duration, such as number of working days.

Example: Duration Per Task

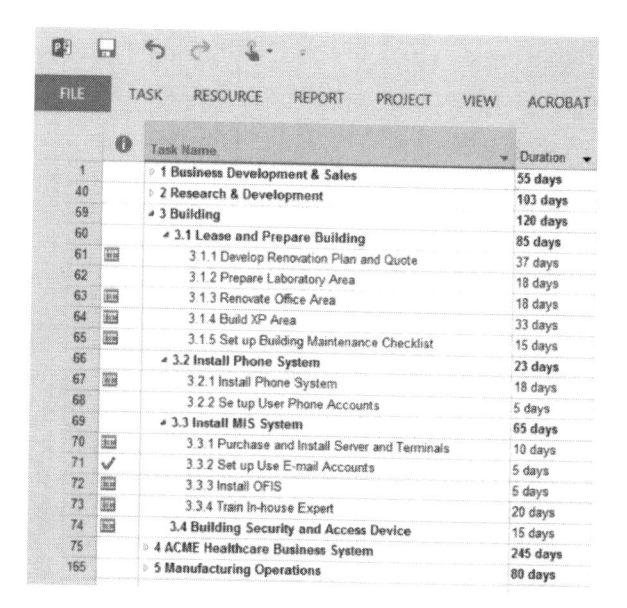

#	Task Name	Duration
1	1 Business Development & Sales	55 days
40	2 Research & Development	103 days
59	3 Building	120 days
60	3.1 Lease and Prepare Building	85 days
61	3.1.1 Develop Renovation Plan and Quote	37 days
62	3.1.2 Prepare Laboratory Area	18 days
63	3.1.3 Renovate Office Area	18 days
64	3.1.4 Build XP Area	33 days
65	3.1.5 Set up Building Maintenance Checklist	15 days
66	3.2 Install Phone System	23 days
67	3.2.1 Install Phone System	18 days
68	3.2.2 Se tup User Phone Accounts	5 days
69	3.3 Install MIS System	65 days
70	3.3.1 Purchase and Install Server and Terminals	10 days
71	3.3.2 Set up Use E-mail Accounts	5 days
72	3.3.3 Install OFIS	5 days
73	3.3.4 Train In-house Expert	20 days
74	3.4 Building Security and Access Device	15 days
75	4 ACME Healthcare Business System	245 days
165	5 Manufacturing Operations	80 days

Step 6: Identify the Predecessor Tasks

For each task, identify prerequisite tasks. These are tasks that need to be completed prior to starting the next task. Some tasks may not have a predecessor, or multiple tasks may be identified as predecessors.

Example: Identification of Predecessor Tasks

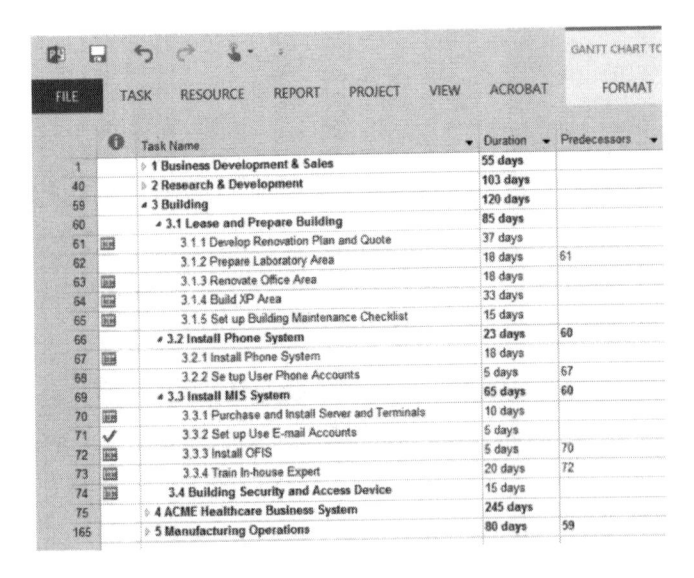

	Task Name	Duration	Predecessors
1	▷ 1 Business Development & Sales	55 days	
40	▷ 2 Research & Development	103 days	
59	▲ 3 Building	120 days	
60	▲ 3.1 Lease and Prepare Building	85 days	
61	3.1.1 Develop Renovation Plan and Quote	37 days	
62	3.1.2 Prepare Laboratory Area	18 days	61
63	3.1.3 Renovate Office Area	18 days	
64	3.1.4 Build XP Area	33 days	
65	3.1.5 Set up Building Maintenance Checklist	15 days	
66	▲ 3.2 Install Phone System	23 days	60
67	3.2.1 Install Phone System	18 days	
68	3.2.2 Se tup User Phone Accounts	5 days	67
69	▲ 3.3 Install MIS System	65 days	60
70	3.3.1 Purchase and Install Server and Terminals	10 days	
71	3.3.2 Set up Use E-mail Accounts	5 days	
72	3.3.3 Install OFIS	5 days	70
73	3.3.4 Train In-house Expert	20 days	72
74	3.4 Building Security and Access Device	15 days	
75	▷ 4 ACME Healthcare Business System	245 days	
165	▷ 5 Manufacturing Operations	80 days	59

Step 7: Assign Responsibility

During the assignment of responsibilities, allocate tasks to core project members and other members on the resource list.

Step 8: Determine the Start-Finish Dates

Assign start-finish dates for each task and milestone. Consider the predecessor tasks when assigning dates.

Example: Task Responsibility and Due Dates

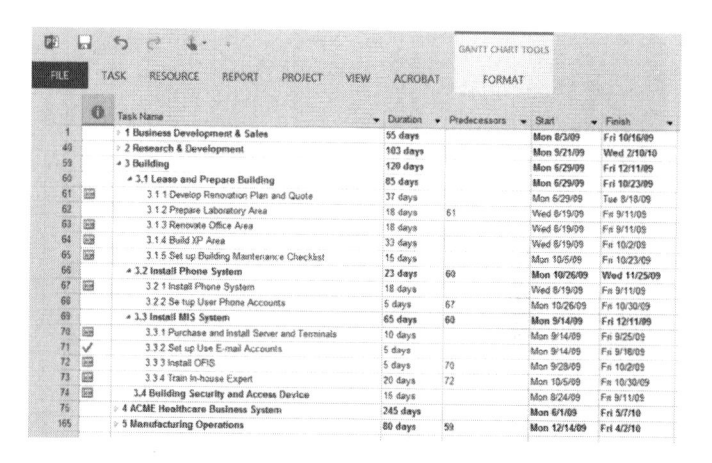

		Task Name	Duration	Predecessors	Start	Finish
1		1 Business Development & Sales	95 days		Mon 8/3/09	Fri 10/16/09
40		2 Research & Development	103 days		Mon 9/21/09	Wed 2/10/10
59		3 Building	120 days		Mon 6/29/09	Fri 12/11/09
60		3.1 Lease and Prepare Building	85 days		Mon 6/29/09	Fri 10/23/09
61		3.1.1 Develop Renovation Plan and Quote	37 days		Mon 6/29/09	Tue 8/18/09
62		3.1.2 Prepare Laboratory Area	18 days	61	Wed 8/19/09	Fri 9/11/09
63		3.1.3 Renovate Office Area	18 days		Wed 8/19/09	Fri 9/11/09
64		3.1.4 Build XP Area	33 days		Wed 8/19/09	Fri 10/2/09
65		3.1.5 Set up Building Maintenance Checklist	15 days		Mon 10/5/09	Fri 10/23/09
66		3.2 Install Phone System	23 days	60	Mon 10/26/09	Wed 11/25/09
67		3.2.1 Install Phone System	18 days		Wed 8/19/09	Fri 9/11/09
68		3.2.2 Set up User Phone Accounts	5 days	67	Mon 10/26/09	Fri 10/30/09
69		3.3 Install MIS System	65 days	60	Mon 9/14/09	Fri 12/11/09
70		3.3.1 Purchase and Install Server and Terminals	10 days		Mon 9/14/09	Fri 9/25/09
71	✓	3.3.2 Set up Use E-mail Accounts	5 days		Mon 9/14/09	Fri 9/18/09
72		3.3.3 Install OFIS	5 days	70	Mon 9/28/09	Fri 10/2/09
73		3.3.4 Train In-house Expert	20 days	72	Mon 10/5/09	Fri 10/30/09
74		3.4 Building Security and Access Device	15 days		Mon 8/24/09	Fri 9/11/09
75		4 ACME Healthcare Business System	245 days		Mon 6/1/09	Fri 5/7/10
165		5 Manufacturing Operations	80 days	59	Mon 12/14/09	Fri 4/2/10

Step 9: Route the Project Plan for Approval

Route the project plan for review, feedback, and approval. Validate the project plan to assure alignment to the strategic plan or organizational goal.

Project Summary Report

In this section, a report summary is created for each project. It includes a set of performance metrics, accomplishments from the previous week, plan for the week, and identification of issues encountered. Below is an example of a simple project summary report.

Example: Project Summary Report

Project Name		Project Leader	
Description & Scope		Target Date	

Performance Measures

#	Item	Week Actual	Week Plan	Project-to-Date Actual	Project-to-Date Plan	Notes
	Performance to Plan					
	% to Plan					
	Budget					

Highlights Last Week

#	Activity	Who	Due	Notes / Status

Plan for the Week

#	Activity	Who	Due	Notes / Status

Concerns & Issues

#	Issue	Action	Due

Projects Dashboard

When working with multiple projects, a simple dashboard helps identify projects that require closer attention. Set up a board listing all projects as shown below.

Each week, the project leader posts color-coded flags indicating *on time*, *may be late*, or *late* under the Status column. The project leader should also post the percentage of the task completed or another indication that the project is moving forward.

Example: Multiple Project Dashboard

Status	#	Project	Leader	Week of			

Project Planning and Management

Chapter 6: Kaizen Events

Process Overview

A Kaizen event, also known as a Kaizen Blitz, is a fast-and-furious process improvement deployed at a targeted area and scope of work. The Kaizen event process in this chapter follows the plan-do-check-act (PDCA) process-improvement cycle.

Multiple cycles are conducted in each event. The first cycle measures the current state and forms the baseline to validate historical data. In some instances, baseline cycle data may differ significantly from historical data. This is due to higher process compliance along with a phenomenon called the Hawthorne Effect. The Hawthorne Effect occurs when a closely monitored activity causes people to modify their behavior and alters performance data.

Process analysis and improvements are made with data and observations gathered from each cycle. All members of the operational team and support staff review the data, develop an improvement plan, and implement the plan in preparation for the next cycle.

The second cycle will show the largest performance-metric improvements. The succeeding cycles will yield minimal improvements relative to the second cycle. Here is the profile of observed performance improvements for a Kaizen event, with the first cycle as baseline.

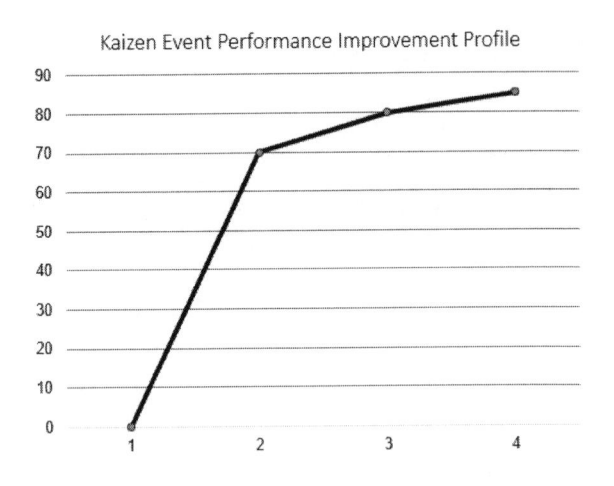

Kaizen Event Performance Improvement Profile

Event Preparation

To sustain long-term effectiveness and compliance, a thorough preparation of all system elements is required.

People: All members of the operational team and support staff are briefed on the Kaizen event's objective, scope, and general plan. Involve all members in the detailed planning, preparation, and implementation. Develop a staffing plan and member responsibilities.

Machines: Create a checklist of fixtures, machines, equipment, and tools. Make sure the items are available for the event.

Materials: Create a master list of parts and materials required. Allocate, identify, and set aside the quantities.

Methods: Develop a big-picture process map showing the general process within the scope of the Kaizen event. Review the current data-collection process, and enhance the process for quick data retrieval if necessary.

Data: Use key performance metrics and compiled data to paint the picture describing the current state and to issue a statement. Compile the master records that will be used for the event. Master records contain the product or service specifications, drawings, and standards. Compile the necessary forms for a product or service-history record.

Rules of the Game
Create a simple list of rules to maintain the integrity of the Kaizen event. The process must propel itself without any artificial effort, guidance, or support.

Stress the importance of people performing the task at a normal pace. Focus on process compliance and not speed.

To highlight bottlenecks and line balance where subassemblies are passed on to multiple workstations, limit the subassemblies completed to two units, one unit at a transfer station and the other at the workstation. This will cause the workstation to stop.

The technical support staff is instructed to step back, observe the process, and not interact or help out during the event cycles.

Here is a summary of the Kaizen event rules:
- Perform the process and functions as specified.
- Execute with a normal pace—do not rush.
- Stop when work-in-process inventory contains two units.
- Support staff should observe and keep their hands off the process.

Implementation Procedure

PDCA: Plan Phase

Step 1: Define the Objective

The objective contains a statement of the current state and the target future state, such as "Improve the service-packet-completion cycle time from six hours to two hours."

Step 2: Gather Current Process Data

Compile and study standards, specifications, historical data, and performance metrics. Draw a process map, and summarize the key points for each main step. Gather process cycle times for each workstation, if necessary.

Step 3: Plan the Kaizen Event

Define the scope of the Kaizen event, outlining the start and end of the process, the products to make or services to provide, and the total number of units to produce.

Identify performance metrics to track the overall system effectiveness and diagnostic measures to monitor details of the process. Examine the current data-collection process, and verify that all performance data are collected. Design a data-collection process, if necessary, to quickly gather new data points.

Step 4: Prepare for Cycle #1

Prepare the work area, and verify that the required materials and equipment are placed in position. Examine the layout of the work area, and mark two locations for work-in-process inventory to signal the station to stop when both locations are filled.

Develop procedures where none are available, or update current procedures that are grossly inaccurate. Verify training competencies, and retrain people if necessary.

Set up the data-collection sheets and performance charts in an area close to the Kaizen event. This area will be used for the entire team to review the data, analyze it, and develop process improvements.

Conduct a trial run of the process to verify that all elements of the system are ready. In a production setting, building two units is sufficient.

PDCA: Do Phase

Step 5: Run Cycle #1 for Baseline Data

Review the rules of the game prior to starting the cycle. Provide last-minute instructions to assure the integrity of the data and the entire event cycle. The team should focus on process compliance.

Collect production data, and have the support staff gather observations pertaining to line balance, equipment or material issues, process compliance, and tempo.

PDCA: Check Phase

Step 6: Examine Quality and Performance

Conduct a thorough examination of the products produced and/or services provided. Document detailed quality and performance outcomes.

Step 7: Prepare Data for Analysis

Compile all data, and present it in both detailed and summary formats. As much as possible, present data in graphs and charts.

Step 8: Analyze the Performance Data

The Kaizen event leader presents the data to all members of the operations staff and support staff. Start with the overall performance metrics, and then drill down to diagnostics measures and detailed data points.

The event leader encourages the participants to collectively identify issues and share observations.

PDCA: Act Phase

Step 9: Implement Corrective Action

Prioritize the performance issues. Develop a corrective-action plan targeted to improve the top performance issues. Engage the operational staff in the development and implementation of the corrective-action process.

PDCA: Plan Phase

Step 10: Prepare for Cycle # 2

Prepare the work area, and verify that the required materials and equipment are placed in position. Update the process map, procedures, and documents affected by the improvements. Conduct training and coaching to ensure compliance with new processes.

Conduct a trial run of the process to verify that all elements of the system are ready. In a production setting, building two units is sufficient.

PDCA: Do Phase

Step 11: Run Cycle #2

Review the rules of the game prior to starting the Kaizen event. Provide last-minute instructions to assure the integrity of the data and the entire event cycle. Have the team focus on process compliance.

Collect production data, and have the support staff gather observations pertaining to line balance, equipment or material issues, process compliance, and tempo.

PDCA: Check Phase

Step 12: Examine Quality and Performance

Conduct a thorough examination of the products produced and/or services provided. Document detailed quality and performance outcomes.

Step 13: Prepare Data for Analysis

Compile all data, and present it in both detailed and summary formats, comparing it to the previous run cycle(s).

Step 14: Analyze the Performance Data

Review the run-cycle data, and compare it to the previous run cycle and the planned objectives. Start with the overall performance metrics, and then drill down to diagnostics measures and detailed data points.

PDCA: Act Phase

Step 15: Implement Corrective Action

Prioritize the performance issues. Develop a corrective-action plan to improve the top performance issues.

PDCA: Next Run Cycle

Continue to run multiple PDCA cycles until the desired performance is achieved.

Chapter 7: Corrective-Action Process

Process Overview

Implementing an effective corrective-action process requires a firm grasp of the facts and identification of the root cause of the nonconformance.

Investigating a nonconformance is a methodical process for collecting data. It forms the foundation of identifying affected lots and formulating the root cause of the issue. In a product nonconformance situation, identifying the suspect lots and isolating them from further distribution is the first course of action.

The design and execution of product-batch and service records are vital elements in a nonconformance investigation. Every detail is a clue to re-creating the process and identifying the root cause.

Developing the corrective action is easy when supported by a solid root-cause analysis. The two-part procedure describes the steps at investigating a nonconformance and the development of a corrective-action plan.

The Nonconformance and Corrective-Action Process

Investigating a Nonconformance or Issue

Step 1: Document Customer Information

Compile data upon receipt of the nonconformance. Determine the type of feedback, if provided by a customer.

WHAT	Feedback Type	___ Internal ___ External ___ FYI ___ Complaint
	Product Number	
	PO Number	
	Job Order Number	
	Quantity of Rejected Product	
WHO	Company	
	Contact Name	
	Contact Title	
	E-mail	
	Phone Number	
WHY	Reason(s) for rejecting the product	
	Specification or Expectation	
WHEN	Discovery Date	
	Time or Shift Number	
HOW	How was rejection found?	
WHERE	Plant Location	
	Department	
	Machine Center	

Step 2: Confirm the Nonconformance

Contact the customer or end-user to confirm the accuracy of the initial data gathered. Collect more details, if necessary. Assure the customer or end-user that an investigation is being conducted and the appropriate course of action will be taken.

Step 3: Implement Immediate Corrective Action

If necessary, formulate and implement an immediate corrective action to contain the spread of the nonconformance.

Action	Responsibility	Due Date	Status

Step 4: Examine Product and Service Records

Product lots and service records are produced in sequence. Gather the records, and develop a sequential list of lots.

Conduct a thorough examination of the product-batch records, service records, line clearance logs, and other documents associated with the area.

Corrective-Action Process

Batch Record

Date	Shift	Dept	Operator	Batch Record Notes

Maintenance Log Review

Date	Shift	Dept	Machine	Maintenance Activity

Step 5: Determine the Affected Lots

Determine if the lots immediately before and after the suspect lot are conforming to the specifications. The form below will clearly identify a pattern of nonconformance.

	Lot Number	Part Number	Conforming?	
-5 Lot Before			Yes	No
-4 Lot Before			Yes	No
-3 Lot Before			Yes	No
-2 Lot Before			Yes	No
-1 Lot Before			Yes	No
Suspect Lot			Yes	No
+1 Lot After			Yes	No
+2 Lot After			Yes	No
+3 Lot After			Yes	No
+4 Lot After			Yes	No
+5 Lot After			Yes	No

Step 6: Quarantine the Affected Lots

Isolate all products in inventory, and determine the whereabouts of products distributed. A lot-traceability process will help expedite the product-recall process.

Isolate and quarantine nonconforming product to avoid contaminating other product lots, and stop the product distribution.

Step 7: Identify the Potential Causes

Create a checklist of elements in the system. Brainstorm a list of all potential causes of the nonconformance. At this point, include all potential causes, even if it is just remotely possible. A qualification process will follow to include or disqualify a potential cause.

A historical compilation of potential root causes can be used as a template to assist in identifying the root cause.

Example Template for Potential Root Causes

		Notes
People	☐ Noncompliance to procedure ☐ Insufficient job knowledge ☐ Other	
Machine	☐ Part or machine failure ☐ Setup and run setting errors ☐ Other	

		Notes
Materials	☐ Nonconforming material ☐ Inconsistent quality ☐ Material change without notice ☐ Other	
Methods	☐ Undocumented procedure ☐ Insufficient details or check frequency ☐ Other	
Data	☐ Missing or incorrect specifications at check sheet ☐ Other	
Environment	☐ Temperature ☐ Humidity ☐ Air quality ☐ Work center line clearance ☐ Other	

Step 8: Describe the Sequence of Events

Develop a potential sequence of events that led to the nonconformance. In some cases, multiple scenarios are developed and ranked according to the probability of occurrence.

Step 9: Identify the Root Cause

Analyze the sequence of events and data gathered to qualify the list of potential causes. By elimination, identify one or multiple root causes.

During the analysis, take advantage of the opportunity to improve the overall effectiveness of the system.

		Notes
People	☐ Noncompliance to procedure	
	☐ Insufficient job knowledge	
	☐ Other	
Machine	☐ Part or machine failure	
	☐ Setup and run setting errors	
	☐ Other	

		Notes
Materials	☐ Nonconforming material	
	☐ Inconsistent quality	
	☐ Material change without notice	
	☐ Other	
Methods	☐ Undocumented procedure	
	☐ Insufficient details or check frequency	
	☐ Other	
Data	☐ Missing or incorrect specifications at check sheet	
	☐ Other	
Environment	☐ Temperature	
	☐ Humidity	
	☐ Air quality	
	☐ Work center line clearance	
	☐ Other	

Corrective-Action Process

Formulating a Corrective-Action Plan

Step 10: Draft a Corrective-Action Plan

Develop a list of potential corrective actions targeting each root cause.

		Action Plan	Notes
People	☐ Noncompliance to procedure	☐ Rewrite or develop procedure ☐ Conduct training ☐ Address performance issue ☐ Add fail-safe system (Poka-Yoke device)	
	☐ Insufficient job knowledge	☐ Conduct training and coaching ☐ Assign OJT Time	
	☐ Other		
Machine	☐ Part or machine failure	☐ Establish part standard ☐ Set up part standard with vendor ☐ Monitor part quality from vendor ☐ Verify effectiveness of setup ☐ Update setup procedure ☐ Verify compliance to maintenance schedule ☐ Update maintenance schedule ☐ Monitor for electrical surges ☐ Install surge protectors ☐ Monitor for fluctuating air pressure ☐ Install air pressure regulator ☐ Conduct training and coaching	
	☐ Set up and run settings	☐ Verify accuracy of procedures ☐ Update procedures ☐ Verify compliance to procedure ☐ Conduct training and coaching	
	☐ Other		
Materials	☐ Inconsistent quality	☐ Establish part standard ☐ Set up part standard with vendor ☐ Require vendor CAR ☐ Monitor part quality from vendor ☐ Conduct Vendor Audit	
	☐ Material change without notice	☐ Establish procedure ☐ Conduct training ☐ Monitor for compliance ☐ Conduct Vendor Audit	
	☐ Other		

Manager's Guide to Lean and Performance

Corrective- Action Plan

		Action Plan	Notes
Methods	☐ Undocumented procedure	☐ Document Procedure ☐ Conduct training and coaching ☐ Update check sheet	
	☐ Insufficient details or check frequency	☐ Document Procedure ☐ Conduct training and coaching ☐ Update check sheet	
	☐ Other		

Data	☐ Missing or incorrect specifications	Customer: ☐ Approach customer for change, send change request form ☐ Update specifications ☐ Update check sheet	
	☐ Other		

Environment	☐ Temperature	☐ Determine standard ☐ Determine actual ☐ Identify plan to attain standard	
	☐ Humidity	☐ Determine standard ☐ Determine actual ☐ Identify plan to attain standard	
	☐ Air quality	☐ Determine standard ☐ Determine actual ☐ Identify plan to attain standard	
	☐ Line Clearance	☐ Determine standard ☐ Determine actual ☐ Identify plan to attain standard	
	☐ Other		

Step 11: List Corrective-Action Plan

Qualify each potential corrective action, and formulate a corrective-action plan.

Action	Responsibility	Due Date	Status

Step 12: Determine the Scope of the Corrective Action

Is the action plan applicable to other parts or departments? Determine if other products, departments, or processes may benefit from the corrective-action plan.

Step 13: Verify the Effectiveness

Examine the effectiveness of the corrective-action plan thirty to sixty days after implementation. Determine if the action plan is preventing the occurrence of the nonconformance. Close the nonconformance file when a corrective-action-effectiveness audit yields a satisfactory outcome.

Chapter 8: Applying Kanban

Managing Inventory and Flow

Kanban (khan-bun) is a visual communication method intended to prompt a buyer or a vendor to send a replenishment order. It is best used for materials kept in stock, also known as inventory items.

The challenge in keeping inventory is to strike a balance at maintaining the least amount of inventory while providing on-time delivery of materials.

In another application, Kanban is used for implementing one-piece-flow manufacturing. Rather than cards, it utilizes physical markings on the floor to signal work centers when to make and stop manufacturing subassemblies.

In a manufacturing line where one work center feeds the other with subassemblies, a designated square area is painted on the floor, called the Kanban Square. As soon as the Kanban Square is filled, the operator stops and moves to another work center. He or she resumes production at the work center when the Kanban Square is empty.

In this chapter, two exclusive Kanban designs are presented for inventory management. These designs are proven effective at significantly reducing inventory levels and creating a stable supply flow between a manufacturing site and its suppliers.

In a fabrication company, the use of Kanban reduced its steel inventory by 55 percent and eliminated material stock-outs. At a medical-device company, raw-material inventory was reduced from a thirty-five-day supply to a three-day supply, and finished-goods inventory was cut from forty-five to seven days. This was achieved while improving on-time delivery metrics.

At a surgical-device-manufacturing cell, Kanban was deployed to balance material flow and was also used as a mechanism to rotate the production staff to work on multiple stations, avoiding injuries caused by repetitive stress syndrome.

Role of Kanban

A Kanban system can help a Material Requirements Planning (MRP) system track expensed items. Consumable supplies, such as work gloves or safety glasses, are examples of expensed items. These are not tracked as inventory items, and no automated tracking system is in place to trigger a reorder.

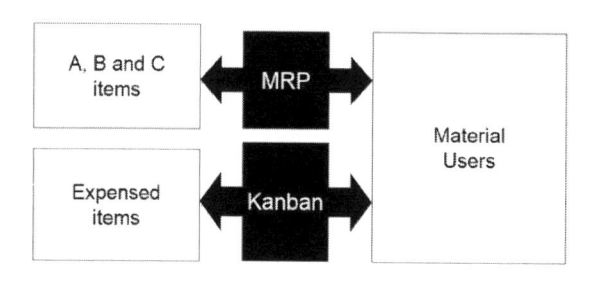

```
┌──────────────┐     ┌─────┐     ┌──────────────┐
│  A, B and C  │ ◄── │ MRP │ ──► │              │
│    items     │     └─────┘     │   Material   │
└──────────────┘                 │    Users     │
┌──────────────┐   ┌────────┐    │              │
│   Expensed   │◄──│ Kanban │──► │              │
│    items     │   └────────┘    └──────────────┘
└──────────────┘
```

Materials in ERP are ranked based on cost and importance for tracking inventory. High-priced raw-material items are designated as "A" items.

In advanced Kanban implementations, the role of Kanban can shift to managing "C" and even "B" inventory items.

This cuts down the number of items in the MRP system. The materials department can focus on managing high-cost items or items with very long delivery lead times.

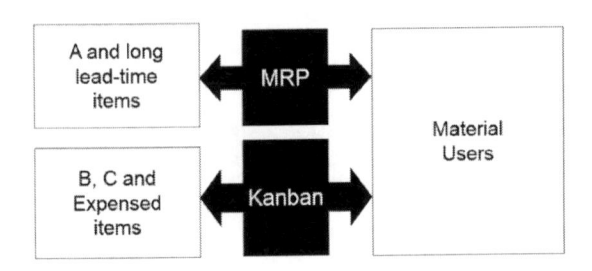

Kanban Board

Inventory is visually managed using a Kanban board. Trigger cards are hung on the board representing all materials in a work cell. Stock-Keeping Unit (SKU) cards are placed on every material. As the material is used, the SKU cards are placed under the corresponding Trigger card. An example is shown below.

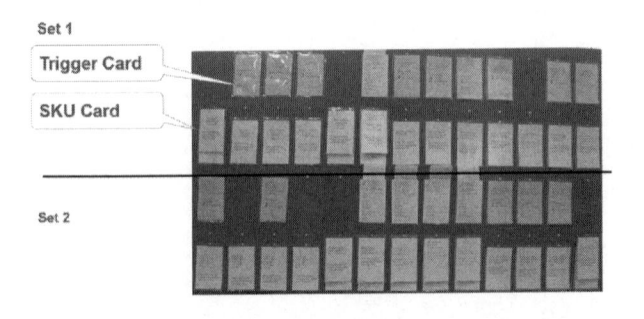

Inventory responsibility is delegated to the end-users of materials. It is typical to expect each work center to use Kanban boards to manage all materials used in its area.

Kanban Cards

The Kanban designs presented in this chapter utilize (1) Trigger cards and (2) Stock-Keeping Unit (SKU) cards.

A Trigger card is a placeholder on the Kanban board containing material data and instructions when to trigger a resupply. The Trigger card is color-coded to differentiate between a raw-material item and a finished product. The reorder signal is standardized to two SKU cards.

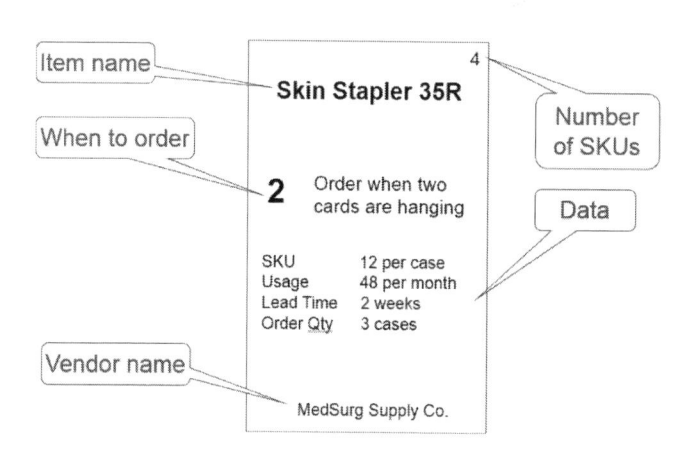

```
Item name ──────┐      ┌─────────── 4
                │  Skin Stapler 35R          Number
When to order ──┤                            of SKUs
                │   2  Order when two
                │      cards are hanging     Data
                │
                │  SKU        12 per case
                │  Usage      48 per month
                │  Lead Time  2 weeks
                │  Order Qty  3 cases
Vendor name ────┤
                │     MedSurg Supply Co.
```

Applying Kanban

The back side of the Trigger card holds the reorder form. It contains part information, standard release specifications, release history, vendor information, and a vendor confirmation.

Supply Order-Release Form
Healthcare Provider Medical Center
ATTN: Jane Smith
Fax (269) 344-4561   Phone (269) 344-5500
Email Jane.Smith@healthcareprovider.org

Item Number	**35-89156**
Standard Release	**36 units**
Item Name	**Skin Stapler 35 R**
Standard Release	**36 units**
Lead Time	**2 weeks from release date**

Release Date	By	Delivery Date

Vendor Information
MedSurg Supply Co.   Blanket PO# 987-01
ATTN Gregory Jones
Fax (847) 866-7800   Phone (800) 665-1000 ext 256
Email GJones@MSSC.com

Delivery Specification
Deliver to arrive at Healthcare Provider Medical Center receiving dock 3 no sooner than 1 week or later than 2 weeks of release date

Vendor Confirmation
Will meet delivery time?	Yes	No
Will supply requested quantity?	Yes	No
If No, shipment size		_____ units

Processed by _____   Date _____

This form is scanned or photocopied and sent to the vendor to release a shipment for delivery on the target delivery date. The vendor, in return, sends a confirmation indicating its intent to comply with the delivery specifications. Delivering the material late or early will impact the integrity of the Kanban system.

In advanced Kanban implementations, the role of purchasing shifts to strategic sourcing, and the process for releasing materials is delegated to production operators or material end-users.

An SKU card indicates the standard quantity of materials determined by a design specification unique to the item. An SKU card is attached to each packaged material and is removed before the first item of the SKU is pulled for use.

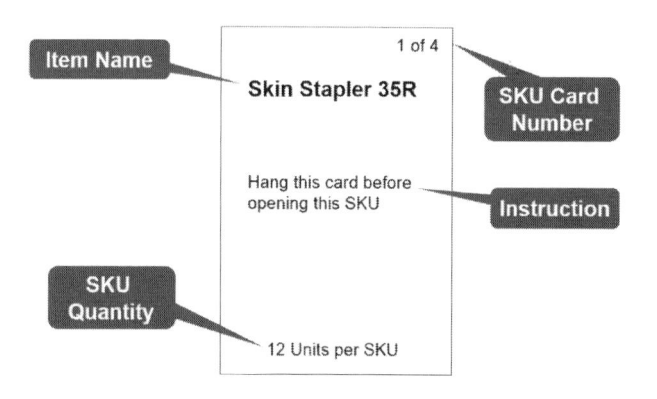

Item Name

1 of 4
Skin Stapler 35R

SKU Card Number

Hang this card before opening this SKU

Instruction

SKU Quantity

12 Units per SKU

Two-Bin Kanban System Design

This is the easiest system for managing supply items or low-cost, small-footprint inventory items. It's also very effective.

In a two-bin Kanban system, two Kanban squares are set up. Each square contains materials that will last twice as long as the requirements of the delivery lead-time duration.

For example, if the delivery lead time is one week and one hundred units are used in one week, the Kanban square will have 2 weeks x 100 units per week = 200 units.

Two-Bin System Setup Procedure

Step 1: Examine material usage history.

Step 2: Determine the reorder lead time. Determine a lead time with the highest supplier compliance. The shorter delivery lead times equate to less inventory quantities.

Step 3: Calculate material usage equivalent to the lead-time duration.

Step 4: Calculate the SKU quantity (it equals two times the lead time material requirements).

Step 5: Create the Trigger card, and set it up on the Kanban board.

Step 6: Designate a location for two Kanban squares. Paint or use floor tape to mark each storage location, and label it with the intended material identification.

Step 7: Attach a SKU card to each stock-keeping unit.

Step 8: Instruct users to hang the SKU card when taking the first material unit from the stock-keeping unit.

Applying Kanban

Step 9: Instruct users to process the reorder form when two SKU cards are hanging on the Kanban board.

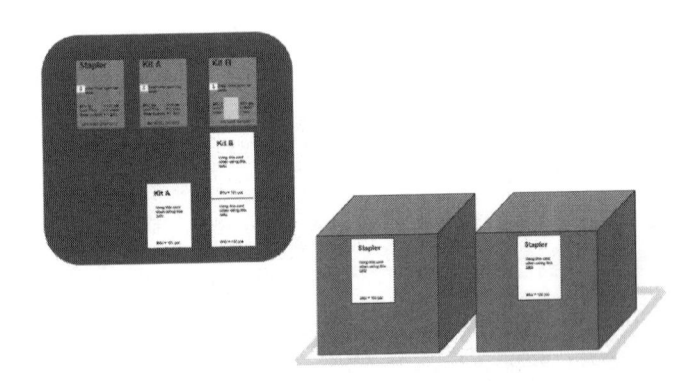

Advanced-Card-System Design

The advanced card system is best used for A, B, and C material types with lead times of less than five weeks. The Trigger card and the number of SKU cards to reorder remain the same as with the two-bin system design. However, the number of SKU cards used per item is between three and eight.

In determining the appropriate number of SKU cards, a logical SKU quantity needs to be determined. This can be a box, case, skid, row of skids, or—in some extreme applications—a warehouse.

SKU cards are segmented in three categories: (i) Cycle SKU, (ii) Lead Time SKUs, and (iii) Safety SKUs. The Cycle SKU has an empirical value of one. This is based on experimentation and experience during the design process. The Lead Time SKUs are determined based on the quantity of materials used during the lead time. The Safety SKUs are intended as "buffer inventories" to absorb supply-chain variability.

Applying Kanban

Advanced-Card-System Setup Procedure

Step 1: Collect material data. Determine the material usage, supplier delivery lead time, and stock-keeping unit configuration.

Item	Bladeless Trocars B12LT
Usage	2,000 units per month
Lead Time	2 weeks
SKU	500 units per skid
Safety Stock	1 week

Step 2: Calculate the Lead Time SKUs.

Number of SKUs consumed during the delivery lead time period

Usage	2,000 units per month or
	4 SKU per month or 1 SKU per week
Lead Time	2 weeks
SKU	500 units per skid

Lead Time SKU = 2 SKUs

Step 3: Calculate the Safety SKUs.

Equivalent number of SKUs calculated for Safety Stock

Usage	2,000 units per month or
	4 SKU per month or 1 SKU per week
SKU	500 units per skid
Safety Stock	1 week

Safety SKU = 1 SKU

Step 4: Cycle SKU = 1

Step 5: Calculate the total number of SKU cards.

> Total number of SKU Cards
> a. Cycle SKU   1
> b. Lead Time SKU   2
> c. Safety SKU   1
>
> Total = **4**

Step 6: Increase the SKU quantities if the total number of SKU cards is greater than eight.

Step 7: Create the Trigger and SKU cards.

Step 8: Set up the Kanban board.

Step 9: Set up the material for Kanban.

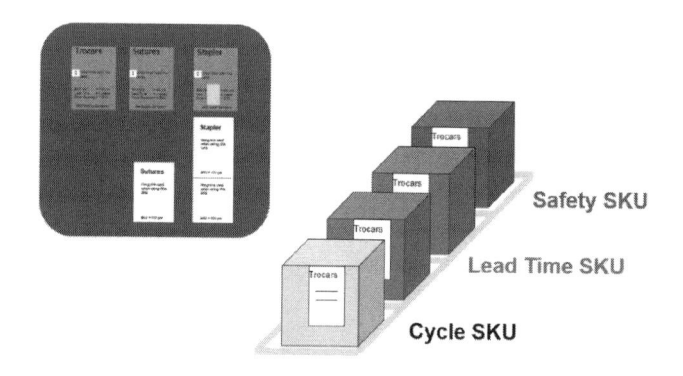

Reorder Procedure

Step 1: Hang the SKU card when using the first item from the Stock-Keeping Unit.

Step 2: If the SKU card is the second card hung on the Kanban board, reorder the material.

Step 3: Complete the reorder form.

Step 4: Photocopy the reorder form located on the back of the Trigger card.

Step 5: Send the form to the supplier via fax or e-mail.

Step 6: Fold the completed form, and insert it in the pocket behind the Trigger card.

Step 7: Hang the Trigger card back on the Kanban board with the reorder form showing.

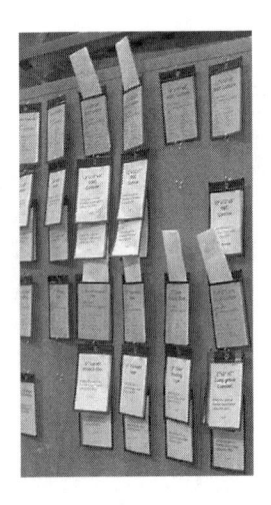

Receiving Procedure

Step 1: Move the incoming materials to the Kanban area.

Step 2: Get the corresponding SKU cards from the Kanban board.

Step 3: Remove the photocopied reorder form.

Step 4: Flip the Trigger card to show the front.

Step 3: Place the SKU cards on the incoming material.

Step 4: Move the Safety SKU or remaining material to the front of the Kanban square.

Step 5: Place the incoming material at the back of the Kanban square.

Applying Kanban

Chapter 9: Bottom-up Performance Reviews

Process Overview

Developing strategic initiatives flows through a top-down cascade, starting from the strategic level and going down to the tactical and operational levels. Performance reviews, on the other hand, require a bottom-up approach.

In a bottom-up approach, work teams are highly regimented and disciplined on working closely with a support staff. This approach requires the establishment of performance-driven work teams and a technical-support-staff structure.

Building a performance-driven and autonomous organization requires a methodical process, guided by a set of performance metrics and a routine performance-review process that cascades from the bottom up.

Bottom-up Performance Reviews

The performance-review structure looks like an upside-down organizational chart as shown below.

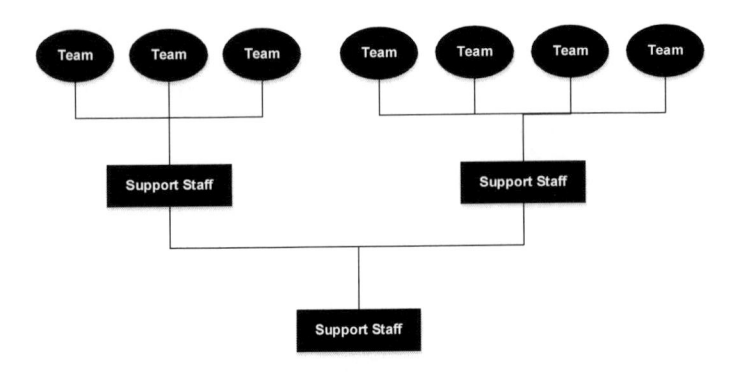

In this structure, work teams review day-to-day diagnostic measures and identify issues that slow down or stop the team from achieving its objectives. Each team is represented by a team leader who provides a report summary to the support staff. The support staff reviews team performance on a routine basis and provides support so teams can achieve their objectives.

Technical Support Staff

The technical support staff is led by the department manager and is complemented by a group of specialists in areas such as quality, purchasing, engineering, and maintenance.

Leading the agenda are the team leaders. They present performance data and identify issues that require technical support. The department manager provides leadership at coordinating the swift completion of action items.

Performance Metrics

Team leaders present performance data in the order of the Input-Process-Output flow covering safety, quality, delivery, and cost metrics.

The department manager and the technical support staff in turn present the overall department metrics, including metrics that demonstrate the effectiveness at supporting the work teams.

Performance metrics for support-staff effectiveness include:

- Issues
  - Received
  - Addressed
  - Oldest Open

- Suggestions
  - Received
  - Implemented
  - Oldest Open

- Nonconformances
  - Received
  - Corrective Actions Completed
  - Oldest Open

Support-Staff Performance Reviews

Performance reviews are scheduled on a routine basis. The department manager develops a list of backup facilitators to assure that the meeting review proceeds as scheduled.

The frequency ranges from daily to weekly. It is also best to schedule the routine meetings before the strategic-level department performance review. This will enable the department manager to utilize the support-staff meeting as the main source of supporting data and prepare for the next-level performance review.

Example Agenda

1. Each Team
    a. Performance review
    b. New issues and concerns
    c. Follow-up on issues and concerns
2. Action Item
    a. New items
    b. Review of open items
3. Support-Staff Performance-Metrics Review

The support-staff performance review starts promptly with a time limit of thirty minutes. Problem-solving activities need to be scheduled separately.

Department Manager as System Administrator

When work teams are formed, the role of the manager changes dramatically. The manager focuses on the delivery of resources, setting goals, and letting the work teams perform.

The organization must coach the department manager on how to utilize team leaders at managing the day-to-day activities. This will reposition the department manager as a "system" administrator, a stepped-back role at monitoring the bigger picture. In this role, the manager monitors the availability of resources, the process compliance of suppliers, and overall system performance.

The first two hours of a work shift is the most critical time of the day. It sets the tone for the day, be it good or bad. The manager and the technical support staff must be on the operations floor monitoring all elements, making sure that they all work together. No meetings should be scheduled during this critical time frame. The all-out effort is to set the drum beat for the shift.

The change in a manager's focus will provide big benefits to the entire organization. Imagine all resource elements delivered on time and performing as expected. This situation eliminates the firefighting mode that most managers seem to assume as normal day-to-day occurrences.

A Common Goal Builds Teamwork

Organizing a team is the easy part. Creating teamwork for self-sufficiency comes with these steps:

1. Identify a set of performance objectives.
2. Define the roles and responsibilities of each member.
3. Train and coach each person to perform his or her tasks.
4. Observe and collect performance data.
5. Present performance feedback.
6. Provide support to improve the process.

The Common Goal

Identifying performance metrics and diagnostics measures is similar to building an instrument panel that monitors the status of supplier performance, team performance, and customer feedback.

In any system, the phases in the process can be simply defined as Input-Process-Output. Suppliers provide all of the resources needed for the team to function in the Input phase. The work team, along with equipment and methods, is in the Process phase. In the Output phase, customers receive the product and services produced by a work team.

Within each phase of Input-Process-Output, there are broad goal categories of safety, quality, delivery, cost, and continuous improvement.

The continuous-improvement category monitors the effort to improve existing systems and procedures such as suggestions, procedure writing, training, and system audits.

A performance-measure planning matrix is used to list all potential performance metrics and diagnostics measures. It references the Input-

Process-Output process and the broad goal categories of safety, quality, delivery, and cost.

Example Performance-Measure Planning Matrix

	Input Supplier	**Process** Team	**Output** Finished Product
Safety	Hazardous material leaks	Accidents Near misses	Stack height compliance
Quality	Defects received	Defects produced	Defects shipped
Delivery	On-Time delivery	Schedule compliance	On-Time delivery
Cost	Purchase price variance	Productivity	Purchase price variance
Continuous Improvement	NCR-CAR	NCR-CAR Suggestions	NCR-CAR

Identify as many performance measures as you can. Then select six to eight key performance measures to monitor team performance.

Providing Team-Performance Feedback

Performance measures must be easy to gather, present, and understand. Charting is an effective method of presenting data to a team. Every chart must indicate the performance objective. The historical average may be considered as the standard or goal. The standards will clearly indicate the common goal and easily tell if performance data is below or above the expected level.

The department manager will have to coach the team to continually ask, "What made us perform *below* or *above* the expected level?" Obviously, you want to avoid unfavorable performance.

For favorable variances, the team should also ask, "How can we continue to perform above the goal line?"

Delegating Work-Team Leadership

An organization can assign either a team leader or team representative to manage the day-to-day activities of a work team.

A team leader is a position that is a step higher than the members of the team. A team representative, on the other hand, is a temporary assignment to a team member for a period of at least three months.

One benefit of the team-representative approach is the opportunity for all team members to learn and experience a leadership position. Some companies use this in the initial training process when introducing the work-team structure. A permanent team-leader position may be implemented after the entire team goes through a full rotation.

Both options can work effectively. Make sure the team leader has an assigned backup person. For the team-representative option, make sure the member is assigned for on-boarding or training.

Role of the Team Leader

The team leader will perform the following tasks:

- Collect and review performance data.
- Make sure every member actively participates in team meetings and activities.
- Provide an objective assessment.
- Align team focus to goals and objectives.
- Coordinate feedback for suggestions, concerns, and issues.

Routine Team Performance Reviews

A team-meeting area is set up so the team can review performance, plan activities, and identify issues. A communications board is installed to hold staffing and vacation plans, performance indicators, the production schedule, and other information to help the team plan and achieve its goals.

Guided by an agenda and procedure, the team leader conducts the meeting on time and within a fifteen-minute time limit. Ideally, the meeting is scheduled at the start of the shift to set the tone for the day. The agenda will routinely cover the following items:

1. Staffing and vacation plans
2. Yesterday's performance
3. Plan for the day
4. Critical materials
5. Concerns, issues, and suggestions

The team leader coordinates the identification of issues and facilitates issue validation with the team. Quick problem-solving activities are discussed in this short team meeting. Issue analysis, problem solving, corrective-action-plan development, and other more time-consuming activities are scheduled in a separate session.

Resolution of issues will mainly take place at the team level. Issues that require technical support and additional resources will be escalated to the support staff.

Bottom-up Performance Reviews

Chapter 10: Developing Self-Sufficiency

Manage Operations through Work Teams

Managers must position themselves at a vantage point from which they can view the bigger picture of the business system or manufacturing system. This will maximize the manager's influence on overall performance. Managing forty people in a department can be a chore, but managing five team leaders is so much easier.

Work teams can be formed as either functional teams or product or service teams. A functional team is a natural grouping of people performing similar tasks or functions. A product or service team has a clear objective of building products or providing a service. Often, this type of work team is more diverse and is spread throughout the building.

Building the Support Structure

If people are spread out in a large area where one or two people work at a work center, it may be difficult to group people into work teams. Try the steps below to define work teams.

1. Draw a flow diagram of the process.

2. Identify segments in the process, either by function, subassembly, or machine centers.

3. Identify the number of people in each segment.

4. Group people in teams of no more than eight members. Teams of more than eight will demand more oversight and structure.

The Supervisor Providing Technical Support

Supervisors experience a big role change when teams are formed. They begin to focus more on setting goals and letting teams operate autonomously. The supervisor's roles in a team environment are to monitor system roadblocks, provide resources, and continuously strive to improve the team's overall performance.

The change in the supervisor's role provides big benefits to both the supervisor and the entire organization. Imagine every element in the system delivered on time and performing as expected. This situation eliminates the firefighting mode that most supervisors seem to assume in response to normal, day-to-day occurrences.

The first two hours of a work shift is the most critical time of the day. It sets the tone for the day, whether good or bad. An all-out effort should be made to set a positive tone by having the supervisors and the technical-support staff assure all elements are working together. No meetings should be scheduled during this critical time frame.

Process Compliance

The primary role and function of a team member is process compliance. Process stability and predictability make it easy to resolve issues. Problems become unnecessarily complex if there is no set pattern to identify root causes and apply an effective corrective action.

Supervisors must remind team members that their job is *not* to make a product or provide a service. Their job is process compliance. Process compliance ensures that products and services are delivered with the highest levels of efficiency and customer satisfaction.

A Common Goal Builds Teamwork

Organizing a team is the easy part. Self-sufficiency of a team comes with these steps:

1. Identify a set of performance objectives.
2. Define the roles and responsibilities of each member.
3. Train and coach each person to perform his or her tasks.
4. Observe team members to collect performance data.
5. Present performance feedback.
6. Provide resources and guidance to improve the process.

The Common Goal

Identifying key performance measures is similar to building an instrument panel that indicates the status of the suppliers, team, and customers throughout the entire process.

A process goes through input, process, and output phases. In the input phase, suppliers provide all of the resources for the team to function. Next, the work team performs the process using equipment and methods. In the output phase, customers receive the products and services produced by a work team.

Within each phase are broad goal categories of safety, quality, delivery, cost, and continuous improvement.

The safety category monitors workplace injuries, accidents, near misses, and lost time. Quality looks at process compliance with customer specifications, including dimensional specifications and items that can't be measured objectively, such as cosmetic requirements. The delivery category measures how well an organization complies with customer specified delivery times, quantities, and

Building the Support Structure

quality conformance. A continuous improvement category monitors the continuing efforts to improve existing systems and procedures, such as suggestions, procedure writing, training, and system audits.

Below is a planning matrix for identifying potential performance measures. It blends the input-process-output process and the categories of safety, quality, delivery, and cost.

	Input (supplier)	Process (team)	Output (finished product)
Safety	Hazardous material leaks	Accidents and near misses	Stack height compliance
Quality	Defects received	Defects produced	Defects shipped
Delivery	On-time delivery	Schedule compliance	On-time delivery
Cost	Purchase-price variance	Productivity	Purchase-price variance
Continuous Improvement	NCR-CAR	NCR-CAR suggestions	NCR-CAR

As you begin to develop your own matrix, list as many performance measures as you can. Then select six to eight key performance measures.

Providing Performance Feedback

Key performance measures must be easy to gather, present, and understand. Charting is an effective method of presenting data to a team. In most cases, a manually drawn chart is more practical and easier to manage than a computer-generated chart.

Every chart must indicate the performance objective or expectation. On the first set of charts, use the historical average as the standard or goal. The standards should clearly indicate the common goal and easily communicate whether performance is below or above the expected level.

Coach the team to ask continually, "What made us perform below or above the expected level?" Obviously, we all want to avoid unfavorable performance. In cases when performance exceeds the goal, we need to also ask, "How can we continue to perform above the goal line?"

Delegating Team Leadership

The organization will have to coach the supervisor to examine the business system and manage the department through team leaders and team representatives.

A team can be manged by a team leader or a team representative. A team leader is one level higher than the members of a team and is a permanent job position. Team representative, on the other hand, is a temporary assignment to a team member, for a period of at least three months. Both options can work effectively.

A team leader should have an assigned backup person to ensure process continuity when the he or she is not available.

If your organization chooses the team representative option, a team member should be assigned for onboarding or training. Soon after assigning a team representative, the former team representatives can be assigned the backup role.

Moving forward, the terms *team representative* and *team leader* will be used interchangeably.

Selecting a Team Leader

A team leader must be able to motivate a team to focus on the process and strive to meet objectives. Leadership qualities are needed at the introduction of the team structure. As the process matures, the team-leadership role shifts from being person dependent to process dependent.

Initially, the supervisor should take the team leader role for the first six to eight weeks. During this time, he or she can monitor the process and make adjustments to fit the department's needs. This is also the best time to train and coach the team leader.

Role of the Team Leader

The team leader will perform the following tasks:

- Collect and review performance data.
- Make sure every member actively participates in team meetings and activities.
- Provide an objective assessment of performance outcomes.
- Align team focus with goals and objectives.
- Coordinate feedback for suggestions, concerns, and issues.

Routine Performance Review

A meeting area should be set up as the communications center, and a bulletin board should be installed to display vacation plans, performance indicators, production schedules, and other information to help the team plan and achieve its goals. The meeting area must be close to the work area. Noise level and lighting should be considered to ensure that an effective meeting can be conducted there.

Guided by an agenda and procedure, the team leader should conduct each meeting on time and within a fifteen-minute time limit. Ideally, meetings should be scheduled at the start of a shift to set the tone for the day. The agenda will routinely cover the following items:

1. Staffing and vacation plan
2. The previous day's performance
3. Plan for the day
4. Critical materials
5. Concerns, issues, and suggestions

The team leader should coordinate the identification of issues that slow down the team or stop it from achieving its goals. All issues should then be validated by the team, and a proposed corrective action should be developed and implemented.

Long problem-solving sessions are to be scheduled outside the routine team meetings. Only quick problem-solving activities should be discussed in the fifteen-minute team meeting.

Resolution of issues will occur mainly at the team level. However, issues that require technical support and additional resources should be directed to the support staff.

Building the Support Structure

Step-by-Step Procedures
Developing Self-Sufficiency

Building the Support Structure

Creating the Team Structure

Instructions

1. Define the team's purpose and objectives.
2. Select a team name.
3. Schedule the routine team meeting. For the operations staff, a daily performance review scheduled at the start of the shift is recommended because the meeting sets the tone for the rest of the shift.
4. List team members. This will be their home team. They may work temporarily in other departments, but this is where they will attend the daily meetings.
5. Define the team leader's roles and duties of the team leader.
6. Select the team leader.
7. Select the backup team leader.
8. Create a roster of employees.
9. Route the team roster to all department employees and managers for feedback and approval.

Identifying Performance Measures

Instructions

1. Identify the customers and suppliers.
2. Use the planning matrix to identify potential performance measures.

	Input (supplier)	Process (team)	Output (finished product)
Safety	Hazardous material leaks	Accidents and near misses	Stack height compliance
Quality	Defects received	Defects produced	Defects shipped
Delivery	On-time delivery	Schedule compliance	On-time delivery
Cost	Purchase-price variance	Productivity	Purchase-price variance
Continuous Improvement	NCR-CAR	NCR-CAR Suggestions 5S score	NCR-CAR

3. Choose no more than eight measurements that represent the team's overall performance.
4. Add scorecards for issue resolution and suggestions.
5. Define each performance measure and sources of data.
6. Route the data definitions to the next-level manager for feedback and approval.
7. Continually review relevance of performance measures.

Collecting Performance Data

Instructions

1. Develop a simple data-collection process for new key performance measures. When possible, the team should collect the data. This will increase ownership of performance data and decrease dependence on the support staff.
2. Create data-collection forms, if necessary.
3. Designate a central location for team members to submit data-collection forms.
4. Create a tally sheet or spreadsheet on which the team leader can compile the data.
5. Write a detailed procedure for how to collect and tally the data using the forms.
6. Train the team on the data-collection process.
7. For two weeks, test the data-collection process for accuracy and timeliness.
8. Improve the data-collection process, if necessary.
9. Integrate the data-collection process into the daily work routine.

Setting Up the Meeting Area

Instructions

1. Purchase a board (a four-by-eight pinboard works well). Additional boards may be needed as the team progresses at using visual management tools.

2. Select a meeting area large enough for the team board and team members. Ensure that a clock can be seen from the meeting area.

3. Organize and clean the meeting area. Remove unnecessary items or postings. Ensure that the area is well lit and quiet enough for a meeting.

4. Mount the pinboard on the wall or on a movable stand.

5. Mark and label the area with the team name. Mark it with floor tape if in a production area.

6. Post team information such as calendars, production and staffing schedules, pictures of team members, and so on.

7. Post temporary notices, indicating the expiration date in the corner of each.

Displaying Performance Data

Instructions

1. Choose a time frame for each performance item (daily, weekly, or monthly).

2. Choose a chart type for each measurement (bar, line, stacked bar, combination, or custom).

3. Standardize the use of color, such as green for actual values and a black line for the goal.

4. Create a chart template for each performance measure.

5. Copy charts onto cardstock to keep the markers from bleeding onto the pinboard and to prevent paper warping due to humidity changes.

6. Write the team name, time period, and legend on each chart.

7. Label the chart index, making sure the data average is about 75 percent of the total chart height.

8. Chart the performance data. Be sure to write in the value of any data point that goes beyond the top of the scale. Do not draw above the charting boundary.

Manager's Guide to Lean and Performance

Example Daily Chart

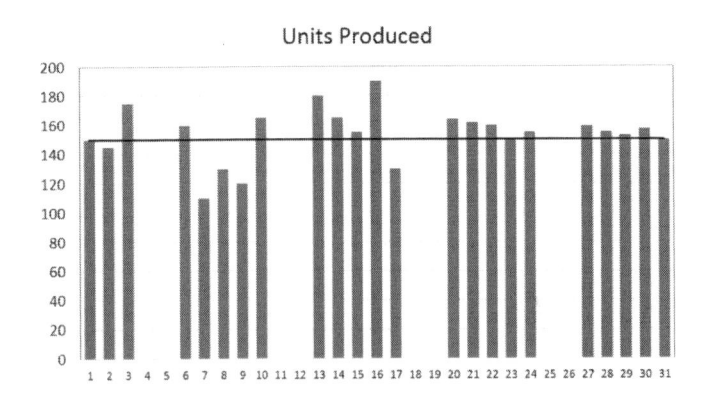

Units Produced

Example Monthly Chart

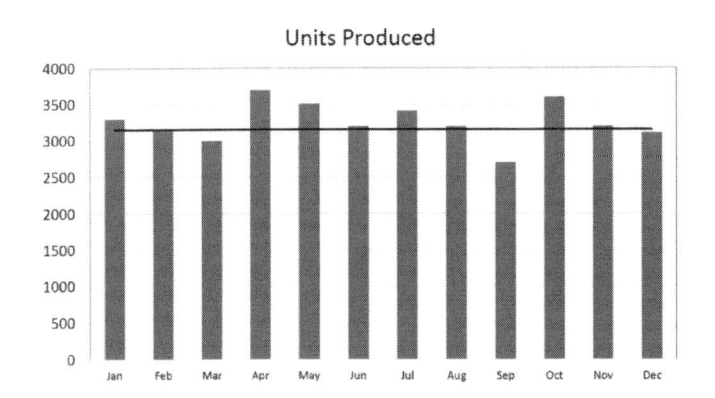

Units Produced

Setting Performance Goals

Instructions

1. Gather and examine historical data.
2. Schedule a meeting with the team leaders, department supervisor, and department manager.
3. Inspect the monthly charts with the team leaders, department supervisor, and department manager. Look for trends and relationships.
4. Calculate the historical average of each chart. Reference the team's tally sheet.
5. Set goals to match company objectives.
6. Determine the impact of these goals on financial, operational, and company goals. Link the monthly goals to budgets, staffing levels, capacity, and production objectives.
7. Create a formal action plan for any goal that is significantly different from its current value.
8. Set a goal for all monthly charts, including Suggestions Received & Implemented and Workplace Organization.
9. Set a goal for each weekly chart by dividing the monthly goal by four.
10. Set a goal for each daily chart by dividing the monthly goal by the average number of days worked.

11. Mark the performance goal on the chart with a black horizontal line. The line should span the entire width of the chart. Use colored lines if there are multiple goals on one chart.
12. Write the exact value of each goal on its axis.
13. Record the goals on the agenda.
14. Explain to the team that performance planning takes practice and patience and that the goals will become more accurate and meaningful as the team gains experience using them.
15. During team meetings, discuss differences between the actual data and the goals.

Developing the Meeting Agenda

Instructions

1. Design a section for each of the following:
    a. Staffing and attendance
    b. Performance review
    c. Plan for the day
    d. Follow-up list for critical materials or supplies
    e. Unplanned events
    f. Follow-up list for issues and concerns
    g. Status of suggestions
2. Customize the agenda to include specific team needs.
3. Limit the agenda to two pages so it can be printed on one double-sided agenda form.

Conducting a Team Meeting

Instructions

1. Go to the meeting area about five minutes before the scheduled meeting.
2. Review the agenda for accuracy and completeness.
3. Position yourself on the left side of the team board.
4. Coach members to form a single-layer semicircle around the team board as they come into the meeting area.
5. Start the meeting on time by greeting the team with a standard greeting, such as "Welcome, everyone" or "Good morning. Let us start."
6. Look around to review attendance, and note any unplanned absence or tardiness. Identify members who are on planned vacations, on reassignments, or in training.
7. Ask the team for updates on upcoming staffing plans, such as vacations, training, or reassignments.
8. Review each performance measure by pointing to the chart. Read the actual value, and compare it to the goal (standard or expected value). Mention whether it is under, on, or over the goal.

9. Ask team members for their feedback when the actual performance value is significantly different from the goal.

10. Determine whether the feedback given by the team needs to be listed in the issues log.

11. Ask team members for any issues with supplies or materials that require attention, including resupply.

12. Ask about any general concerns and issues.

13. Get agreement from the team regarding whether a particular issue is valid for the log sheet.

14. Review the status of issues on the log sheet.

15. Review any new suggestions issued, and determine whether each suggestion is valid. Get agreement from the team to pursue implementation, and document the suggestion on the log sheet for implementation.

16. Before ending the meeting, ask "Are there any other concerns or issues?"

17. End the meeting with a decisive statement, such as, "This ends our team meeting. Have a great day!"

Chapter 11: Building the Support Structure

The Technical-Support Staff

Successful implementation of and long-term compliance with processes requires an infrastructure that encourages self-sufficient work teams. Work teams need help addressing issues and implementing process improvements that require technical support and resources.

The technical-support staff is typically led by the department supervisor and complemented by a group of specialists in areas such as quality, purchasing, engineering, and maintenance. Leading the agenda are the team leaders, who present performance data, identify issues, and recommend corrective action. The supervisor provides leadership to coordinate and ensure swift completion of corrective actions.

A conference room is typically the designated meeting area for the support staff. Some companies post performance charts on the wall to represent each work team. This makes deviations from the standards easy to identify, with each chart showing the latest team data and the expected level of performance.

The diagram below shows the big-picture view of the team and technical-support structure. Multiple support-staff levels may be deployed; this choice is dictated by the size of the organization.

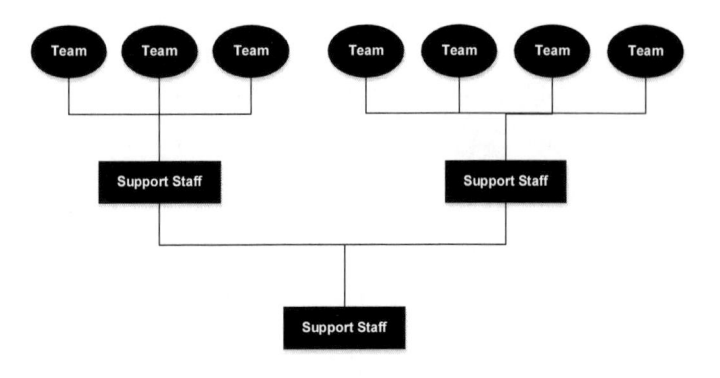

The structure is essentially an upside-down organizational chart. This organizational approach focuses on the needs of the operational teams and ensures conformance to customer requirements. This bottom-up reporting of performance provides quick feedback on the effectiveness of a company's strategy.

Performance Measures

The performance measures of the technical-support staff include the consolidated performance of the work teams. Performance metrics for support-staff effectiveness include the following:

- Issues (received, addressed, oldest open)
- Suggestions (received, implemented, oldest open)
- Nonconformances (received, corrective actions completed, oldest open)

Presenting Performance Data

Presenting from hand-drawn charts posted on the wall may appear technologically backward compared to using computer-generated charts and an overhead projector. However, hand-drawn charts are simple and easy to update before each meeting.

Decide wisely between hand-drawn charts and computer-generated charts. Keep the objective in mind, and use charts to communicate data the quickest and easiest way.

Whatever charting method is used, the supervisor must not be tempted to take over the collection of data and charting of team performance. The entire team must have ownership of the performance data to gain autonomy and self-sufficiency.

The Support-Staff Meeting

The routine support-staff meeting is scheduled based on the data cycle. Often, meaningful data requires a few days or a week. Thus, meeting frequency can range from daily to weekly.

Below is an example of an agenda:
1. Each team
    a. Performance review
    b. New issues and concerns
    c. Follow-up on issues and oncerns
2. Action items
    a. New items
    b. Review of open items
3. Support staff performance metrics review

The meeting should start promptly and conclude within thirty minutes. Problem-solving activities should be scheduled separately. A roster of backup meeting facilitators should be defined to ensure that the meeting proceeds as scheduled.

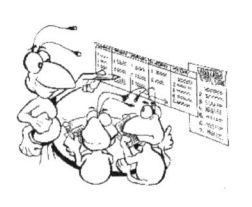

Building the Support Structure

Step-by-Step Procedures
Building the Support Structure

Creating the Support-Staff Structure

Instructions

1. Choose a standard meeting frequency. The meeting should be scheduled to begin two hours after the start of the shift.
2. Identify the support-staff members, including the leaders of the work teams.
3. Define the role and duties of the support-staff team leader.
4. Choose the initial backup team leader, and create a list of succeeding backup leaders.
5. Create a support-staff roster. Use function titles instead of employee names, such as assembly team leader, engineering specialist, and manufacturing manager.
6. Route the support-staff roster to all department employees and managers for feedback and approval.

Identifying Performance Measures

Instructions

Operational Team Review

1. Identify team performance measures for the support staff to review.
2. Identify performance measures for each support-staff function, if needed.

Department Review

1. Identify the department's customers and suppliers.
2. Use the performance-measure planning matrix below.

	Input (supplier)	Process (team)	Output (customer)
Safety	Hazardous material leaks	Accidents and near misses	Stack height compliance
Quality	Defects received	Defects produced	Defects shipped
Delivery	On-time delivery	Schedule compliance	On-time delivery
Cost	Purchase-price variance	Productivity	Purchase-price variance
Continuous Improvement	NCR-CAR	NCR-CAR suggestions 5S score	NCR-CAR

Building the Support Structure

3. Choose a maximum of eight measurements that represent the team's overall performance.
4. Add scorecards for the issue-resolution process and suggestion system.
5. Define each performance measure and sources of data.
6. Route the data definitions to all department employees and managers for feedback and approval.
7. Review key performance measures annually, and update if necessary.

Presenting Performance Measures

Instructions

1. Select a charting time frame (weekly or monthly).
2. Map out a chart for each operational team and support-staff function.
3. Lay out the charts for the department.
4. Choose a chart type for each measurement (bar, line, stacked bar, combination, or custom).
5. Choose colors for each key measurement.
6. Create a chart template for each performance measure.
7. Copy charts onto cardstock to keep the markers from bleeding onto the pinboard and to prevent paper warping due to humidity changes.
8. Write the index on each chart by hand with a dark pen. The data should average about 60 percent of the total chart height.
9. Chart the data with a ruler. Use the narrow tip of a marker for daily bars and the wide tip for monthly bars.
10. Write in the value of any data point that goes off the top of the scale. Do not draw above the charting boundary.
11. Describe unusual highs or lows by placing a note near the data point.

Building the Support Structure

Setting Goals

Instructions

1. Collect data for at least six weeks.
2. Schedule a meeting with the team leader, department supervisor, and department manager. Meet in the team area.
3. Inspect the monthly charts (January through December) during the meeting with the team leader, department supervisor, and department manager. Meet in the team area.
   - Look for trends and relationships between current and past data.
   - Look for trends and relationships among different charts.
   - Calculate the historical average of each performance measure.
4. Set goals to match company objectives. Consider the effects of fiscal-year and calendar-year objectives.
5. Determine the impact of these goals on financial, operational, and company goals.
6. Link monthly goals to financial budgets, staffing levels, capacity, and production objectives.
7. Create a formal action plan for each goal that is significantly different from its current value.
8. Set a goal for all monthly charts, including Suggestions Received & Implemented and Workplace Organization.

9. Set a goal for every weekly chart by dividing the monthly goal by four.
10. Set a goal for each daily chart by dividing the monthly goal by the average number of workdays.
11. Indicate performance goals with a black horizontal line. The line should span the entire width of the chart. Use a ruler. Use colored lines if there are multiple goals.
12. Write the exact value of each goal.
13. Record the goals on a blank meeting agenda. Make copies from this master until the goals change.
14. Explain to the team that performance planning takes practice and patience and that the goals will become more accurate and meaningful as the team gains experience with team performance reviews.
15. Discuss any differences between the actual data and the goals during the team meetings.

Establishing the Meeting Area

Instructions

1. Secure a meeting area.
2. Organize and clean the room as necessary. Remove unnecessary furniture or postings. Silence telephones so they won't ring during the meeting.
3. Mount a pinboard to post performance metrics. Start with one four-by-eight-inch board, and add custom sizes to cover as much wall area as needed.
4. Mount a dry-erase board, a projection screen, and a clock to monitor the length of meeting.
5. Post the name of the support-staff team on the board.
6. Post support-staff information, such as calendars, production schedules, and staffing plans.
7. Post general notices. Indicate the expiration date in the corner of each temporary notice.

Developing the Meeting Agenda

Instructions

1. Design an agenda section to discuss staffing and attendance with each team.
2. Design an agenda section to review yesterday's performance as indicated by each team's key performance measures.
3. Design an agenda section to discuss each team's plan for the day.
4. Design an agenda section to record and follow up on each team's critical material or supply issues. Include a "Done" column to indicate which issues have been resolved.
5. Design an agenda section to discuss each team's unplanned events.
6. Design an agenda section to record and follow up on each team's issues and concerns. Include a "Done" column to indicate which issues have been resolved.
7. Design the agenda so that each team discusses all of their sections before proceeding to the next team.
8. Add a section for support functions next on the agenda, such as Engineering and Purchasing topics. Design an agenda section to discuss suggestions if necessary.
9. Add a general announcements section at the end of the agenda.

Conducting a Support-Staff Meeting

Instructions

1. Start the meeting on time. Do not wait for late members.
2. Discuss any staffing issues with the first team leader indicated on the agenda.
3. Request the previous day's performance measures from the first team leader.
4. Request the previous week's totals and month-to-date numbers on the first day of each week.
5. Request the previous month's totals on the first day of each month.
6. Ask the team leader why the data are unusually good or bad. Ask other support-staff members to get them involved.
7. Record the performance measures on the agenda with supporting notes.
8. Examine the charts to spot trends or relationships.
9. Discuss any differences between actual performance and expected outcomes.
10. Discuss the plan for the day with the first team leader. Discuss scheduling priorities as necessary.
11. Record a brief summary of the plan for the day for the first team.

12. Ask for any new critical issues with raw materials or supplies.

13. Record issues for follow-up. Identify specific items and when they are needed.

14. Discuss the status of any open issues with raw materials or supplies. Follow up on delegated action plans.

15. Check off any issues that have been resolved since the last meeting in the Done column of the agenda.

16. Ask if about any unplanned events since the last meeting. This brief discussion will bring out issues and concerns.

17. Ask for any new issues or concerns. Let the team leader explain the concern for about one minute. If his or her explanation exceeds one minute, explain to all that this discussion must be brief and to the point.

18. Summarize the issue, and then ask if the issue was summarized correctly. Clarify if necessary.

19. Record the issue for follow-up. This reassures the team leader that it will not be forgotten or ignored. Start follow-up items with an action verb.

20. Inform the team members when feedback will be provided. The more important the issue, the quicker the response should be, often by the next support-staff meeting.

21. Delegate follow-up action plans to support-staff members.

Building the Support Structure

22. Discuss the status of any open issues or concerns. Follow up on delegated action plans.

23. In the Done column of the agenda, check off any issues that have been resolved since the last meeting.

24. Delegate problem-solving discussions to the appropriate people. Problem-solving sessions should be scheduled separately.

25. Reschedule sensitive issues. Take time to prepare for the discussion of such issues by validating facts or requesting support from other managers or departments. Encourage guest speakers to attend.

26. Discuss the status of any open projects involving this team. Keep it brief.

27. Ask the team leader for any brief announcements.

28. Repeat discussion of staffing, performance, the plan for the following day, and issues with each team leader.

29. Discuss support-function topics, such as engineering or purchasing issues.

30. Discuss the status of suggestions briefly with the entire support staff.

31. End the meeting on a positive note. Coach the support staff to complete the meeting in twenty to thirty minutes.

Chapter 12: Focus on Compliance

It is difficult to improve a system with inconsistencies spread all over the place. Inconsistencies in following procedures or conforming to standards are also known as nonconformances or noncompliance.

Types of noncompliance include people not following set policies and procedures, machines not being properly maintained or set up, raw materials mixed with defective items, procedures that are impractical, and incomplete data.

Focusing on system compliance establishes the foundation for long-term process improvements. System compliance leads to process stability and predictability, and It is much easier to troubleshoot an issue in a stable and predictable environment.

Below are the system elements and basic resources needed to build system compliance.

Elements	Basic Resource Needs
People	- Baseline qualifications - Training and coaching - Performance objectives and feedback
Machines	- Validation of equipment capabilities - Maintenance schedule - Setup procedures - Operating specifications
Materials	- Material and delivery specifications - Quality assurance inspection protocols
Methods	- Policy and procedures - Guidelines
Data	- Product and/or service specifications - Records

People

Jobs must be appropriately assigned to individuals who have the basic skills and training to perform the required task. Supervisors should keep in mind that *common sense* is a broad term and that there are no books of standards when it comes to common sense.

Training

The best opportunity for an organization to establish a consistent process is during initial training. Effective training involves two distinct parts: (1) the trainer demonstrating the process and (2) the trainee performing the process from memory.

The demonstration part of training includes stating the objective and showing the end results of the process. The trainer provides a step-by-step demonstration of the process while the trainee reads the written procedure aloud. The trainee highlights key points of the process, such as safety or quality issues.

After the demonstration, the trainee performs the process from memory, repeating the key points of the process. The trainer assists the trainee as necessary to perform the process as defined in the written procedure.

After the initial demonstration and trial run, the training may need to be repeated multiple times until the trainee reaches a satisfactory level of proficiency.

Improving Training Compliance

An obsolete procedure or one that is not being followed is traditionally viewed as a training issue. Increasing discipline to follow the written procedure is only half the solution. A comprehensive solution includes the ability of the documentation system to swiftly process changes and suggestions from end users.

Conducting follow-up training sessions will ensure that the process is being followed and that the procedure is up to date. During such sessions, the trainer can reinforce the key points of the procedure and discover potential improvements to the written procedure.

Training Matrix

A training matrix identifies all team members and lists the available job procedures. It identifies the training requirements and training status of each person. A simple training matrix is shown below:

Name	Job 1	Job 2	Job 3	Job 4	Job 5
Joe S.	O	O	*	*	*
Jane A.	*	OK	O	OK	*
Ted O.					OK
Sara C.	OK	OK	O	OK	O

Legend: *   Target item for training
             O   On-the-job training
            OK Proficient

Machines

Current and new equipment must be validated to determine its capabilities and limitations. Analyzing part-to-part inspection data over an extended time can provide insights into the capability and limitations of the equipment. The complexity of the validation process is determined by the criticality of the machine.

Equipment manufacturers provide maintenance schedules to maintain consistent performance. In addition, every organization should develop a series of routine maintenance procedures that will cover end-of-job maintenance; end-of-shift maintenance; end-of-day maintenance; and weekly, monthly, quarterly, and annual maintenance.

Improper machine setup can cause intermittent defects and slowly destroy a piece of equipment. Thus, a setup procedure should be developed to verify each machine's effectiveness at producing parts, throughout the entire production lot.

As much as possible, this process should be engineered for adjusting machine settings. It helps greatly to have visible markings and meters to assist in performing setup and adjustments.

The photograph below shows a pointer used to indicate setup specification.

An inspection plan specifies the quantity of parts that need to be inspected and the frequency of inspection. Plotting the results will show how well the machine produces parts over time. In some cases, a part measurement degrades slowly, and a machine adjustment needs to be made.

Materials

Material standardization starts with the listing of specifications and acceptable tolerances. A full effort should be made to quantify all specifications, including cosmetic or visual requirements. Delivery specifications such as packaging requirements and lead times should also be established to ensure that materials arrive undamaged and on time. These specifications form the baseline, and improvements should be ongoing.

A computer-based inventory system such as materials-requirement planning (MRP) or enterprise-resource planning (ERP) does not cover all types of materials. These systems often focus on high-cost items and not expensed items.

A simple visual inventory-management system can help in managing items not covered by MRP-ERP. A simple signaling method, called "kanban," can be deployed and used along with MRP-ERP systems to improve process compliance.

Once material specifications are on hand, suppliers must fully understand the requirements. A supplier-management process from the purchasing and quality departments can provide objective feedback for suppliers to use in ensuring compliance and implementing improvements.

Methods

Workplace procedures are typically classified by (1) company, (2) department, and (3) job. In addition, a process map can provide a visual representation of how the organization works from start to finish.

A flow diagram should be used, starting with the big-picture view and progressing down to the department level. In addition, a list of main steps, key points, and responsibility can provide more details.

Example of a Procedure Format

Instructions	Main Step	Key Points

Focus on Compliance

Below is a simple example of a process map.

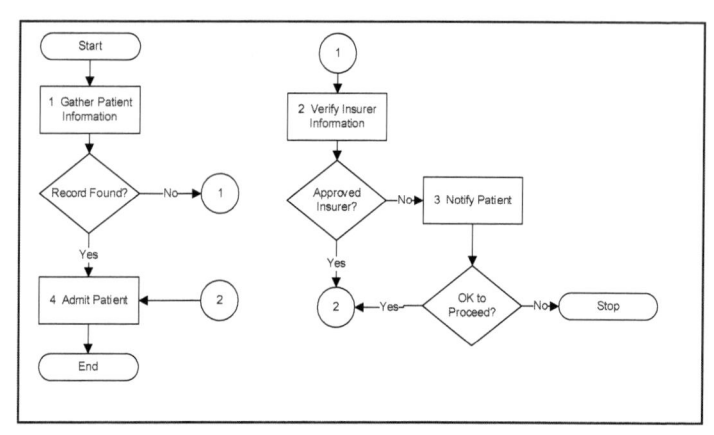

```
Start                                    1
  │                                      │
  ▼                                      ▼
1 Gather Patient                    2 Verify Insurer
  Information                         Information
  │                                      │
  ▼                                      ▼
Record Found? ──No──▶ 1           Approved Insurer? ──No──▶ 3 Notify Patient
  │                                      │                      │
  Yes                                    Yes                     │
  ▼                                      ▼                      ▼
4 Admit Patient ◀── 2              2 ◀──Yes── OK to Proceed? ──No──▶ Stop
  │
  ▼
 End
```

An example format is shown below for main steps, key points, and responsibility.

Main Step	Key Points	Responsibility
1. Gather patient information	• Form DSH-143	Preadmittance
2. Verify insurer information	• Document authorization code • Identify discrepancies	Preadmittance
3. Notify patient	• Identify discrepancies • Provide payment options	Customer service
4. Admit patient	• Enter patient info • Verify diagnosis code • Enter treatment code	Admittance

Data

Data should be treated like raw material. It has to be complete, accurate, and delivered on time. The first set of data is called the *product-service master record*. This contains the specifications and data required to build a product or perform a service, such as specifications, procedures, guidelines, engineering drawings, and photo examples.

Whenever a product is built or a service delivered, data is collected on a product-service history record. In the manufacturing environment, this is known as the *batch record* or *lot record*. In the service environment, it is called, simply, a *service record*. It contains specifications such as work-center number, names, dates, settings, materials used, quantity produced, scrap materials, and quality-inspection records.

Focus on Compliance

Step-by-Step Procedures
Focus on Compliance

Creating a Training System

Instructions

1. Define the purpose of the training system.
2. Choose a procedure format.
3. Create the cover page for the procedure. This includes background information about the process, such as approvals, required materials, and defects prevented.
4. Write a procedure for how to document the current process using work instruction forms and a cover page.
5. Write a procedure for how to route a procedure for feedback and approval.
6. Write a procedure for how to conduct training and improve process compliance.
7. Write a procedure for how to revise a procedure.
8. Train team members.
9. Schedule time for writing procedures and training employees. Use downtime, changeover, breaks, overtime, and the like.
10. Post a procedure-writing to-do list on the team board.
11. Post a training matrix on the team board.

Writing a Work Instruction

Instructions

1. Select a process to document.
2. Select a partner to help you develop the procedure.
3. Go to the location of the actual process.
4. Assign one person to perform the process proficiently and the other to write the instructions legibly.
5. Perform the actual process step by step. Do not modify or improve the current method. Submit process improvements to the team for feedback and approval.
6. Write one instruction for each action step. Include all specifications and critical information within each instruction.
7. Avoid using "and" and "then" to connect multiple instruction. Use "and" only for multiple subjects.
8. Write instructions to complete the process effectively. Leave one blank line between instructions so details can be added later.
9. Write down all instructions necessary to complete the process.
10. Group the instructions into main steps that complete a specific objective or subassembly.

11. Choose a representative verb and subject from within each group of instructions to identify each main step.
12. Write each main step in line with the first instruction of each group.
13. Complete all main steps for the entire process.
14. Identify reference points, directions, specifications, and critical items within each main step.
15. List these items as key points, starting with the main step.
16. Complete key points for all main steps.
17. Draw figures and illustrations for the procedure. Use diagrams, pictures, and flowcharts.
18. Complete the cover page.
19. Review all forms for spelling and legibility.
20. Sign the cover page to indicate your approval.

Example of a Procedure Format

Instructions	Main Step	Key Points

Routing a Procedure for Approval

Instructions

1. Give the completed procedure to knowledgeable team members for review and feedback.
2. Revise the procedure until a consistent team standard is identified.
3. Route the procedure to the support staff for feedback and approval, and revise the procedure to include any support-staff changes.
4. Route the procedure through quality assurance, if necessary.
5. Assign a control number, and indicate the initial revision level.
6. Store one official copy of the procedure in the team area.
7. Archive the original procedure for safekeeping.
8. Add the procedure to the team's training matrix.

Training Procedure

Instructions

1. Schedule time for training at the location of the actual process.
2. Show the end result of the process to the trainee.
3. Review the procedure cover page for background information.
4. Perform the process while the trainee reads the procedure aloud.
5. Assist the trainee as he or she performs the process from memory while verbalizing the main steps and key points.
6. Repeat the training cycle as necessary.
7. Ensure that the trainee can perform the entire process from memory and accurately verbalize all main steps and key points.

Improving Procedure Compliance

Instructions

1. Go to the work center where the process will be performed.

2. Greet the trainee, and indicate your desire to follow up on the previous training and to capture any process improvements he or she may have discovered.

3. Watch the trainee perform the process.

4. Ensure that the trainee completes each main step and is aware of all the key points of the process.

5. Discuss differences between the written procedure and the process being performed by the trainee.

6. Submit process improvements to the team for feedback and approval. Update the procedure as necessary.

7. Retrain or coach the trainee on any process changes.

8. Encourage the trainee to perform the process according to the procedure.

9. Update the team's training matrix.

10. Repeat follow-up training sessions until the trainee is proficient.

Revising a Procedure

Instructions

1. Submit process improvements to the teams and support staff for feedback and approval.
2. Send or give the revised procedure to knowledgeable team members for review and feedback.
3. Revise the procedure until a new team standard has been identified.
4. Route the procedure to the support staff for feedback and approval, and revise the procedure to reflect any support-staff changes.
5. Route the revised procedure through quality assurance, if necessary.
6. Revise the original copy of the procedure, and assign the next revision level.
7. Update the copy of the procedure in the team area. Discard any obsolete procedures distributed in the work area.
8. Archive the old version to maintain a revision history.
9. Update the team's training matrix to indicate that the process has been changed and that training is necessary.

Chapter 13: Managing Improvements

Constant Focus on Compliance

Full compliance with procedures ensures process stability and conformance with performance standards. Process noncompliance produces product defects, inferior customer service, and customer complaints. The nonconformance reporting (NCR) process in a quality system tackles systemic issues, while the issue-resolution process is a proactive step toward resolving issues or concerns that slow down the team or stop it from performing to its fullest capacity.

Performance Data

Setting up an issue-resolution process is simple. Create a log to document each issue, and add the following details:

- Issue noted by
- Issue date
- Resolved date
- Notes

Issue-Resolution Scorecard

A performance scorecard encourages the identification of issues. It also shows overall performance and effectiveness of the team and technical-support structure.

The scorecard shows the following data:

1. Issues identified
2. Issues resolved
3. Issues open
4. Oldest open issue

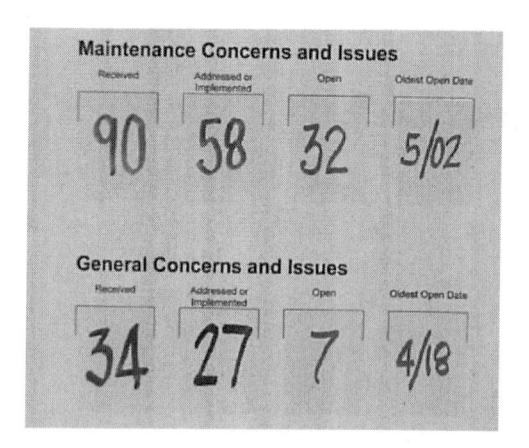

Maintenance Concerns and Issues

Received	Addressed or Implemented	Open	Oldest Open Date
90	58	32	5/02

General Concerns and Issues

Received	Addressed or Implemented	Open	Oldest Open Date
34	27	7	4/18

Employee Suggestion System

A robust suggestion system should be implemented only after launching the issue-resolution process. A suggestion system is focused on improving systems and procedures, while an issue-resolution process is focused on resolving system noncompliance.

A suggestion system is often viewed as a very simple process, but it can be challenging and frustrating. An effective and robust suggestion system requires swift review, implementation, and feedback. Establishing a transparent and visible process encourages employees to actively participate in suggesting and implementing improvements. Posting a scorecard on the number of items identified, the number of implemented suggestions, and the number of open items is simple and effective.

Setting Up the Rules of the Game

Suggestions need to be encouraged to improve safety, quality, delivery, and cost. These factors define the scope of a valid employee suggestion.

Developing a simple process-flow diagram for processing suggestions will make the process transparent and visible to all team members.

Implementation

Before introducing the suggestion system, the work area should be prepared. This includes posting a suggestion flow chart and designating an area for blank and completed forms.

Procedures and guidelines need to be developed for how to process employee suggestions. In addition, the work team's scope, responsibility, and budget need to be defined. Suggestions that require implementation beyond the capabilities and scope of the work team should be directed to the support staff.

Because there will be a flow of suggestions as soon as the system is launched, it is important for the support staff to be trained and ready before the suggestion system is released to the team.

For swift response to suggestions received, the majority of the validation and implementation should be delegated to the team. The work team should have all required resources, such as a budget and time to implement suggestions.

Recognition and Reward

A key to employee satisfaction is having the opportunity to improve the work environment and eliminate inefficiencies. Thus, an organization provides an avenue for job satisfaction by implementing an effective issue-resolution process and an employee suggestion system. Traditional monetary rewards for employee participation are detrimental to teamwork and highly discouraged.Team luncheons or awards recognizing the entire team is an effective approach to reinforce collective team effort.

The issue-resolution process and the suggestion system are tools to help the team and support staff achieve performance objectives. The employee recognition and reward system is embedded in the JPR system.

Managing Improvements

Step-by-Step Procedures
Managing Improvements

Managing Improvements

Tracking Resolution of Issues

Instructions

1. Create an issue log documenting the following:

    - Issue number
    - Description
    - Submitted by
    - Date submitted
    - Resolution notes
    - Resolution date
    - Resolved by

2. Create the scorecard. It should be printed on cardstock and laminated. The scorecard should document the following:

    - Number of issues received
    - Number of issues resolved
    - Number of open issues
    - Date of oldest open issue

3. Hang the issue log in the team meeting area.
4. Train the team to log issues as they observe them.
5. Validate new entries during the team meeting.
6. Decide on the action plan. Set up a problem-solving session, if necessary.
7. Assign team members to resolve the issue.
8. Direct out-of-scope issues to the support staff.
9. Update the scorecard once a week.

Submitting a Suggestion for Improvement

Instructions

1. Develop a suggestion that improves safety, quality, delivery, or cost.
2. Ensure that the suggestion is within the suggestion parameters.
3. Get a blank suggestion form from the team meeting area.
4. Fill out name, date, and team name.
5. Describe the current situation, and illustrate as necessary. Include data and specific details.
6. Describe the proposed suggestion, and illustrate as necessary. Include as much detail as possible, and attach supporting documents.
7. Indicate improvements between the current situation and the proposed suggestion. Use data, and be specific.
8. Present the suggestion to the team during the team meeting.
9. Validate new items in the team meeting. Any new item must improve safety, quality, delivery, or cost and be within the expense budget.
10. Help the contributor modify the suggestion to make it valid, if necessary.

11. Determine whether the team can implement the approved suggestion.
12. Route the approved suggestion to management-support staff, if necessary.

Managing Improvements

Routing a Suggestion to the Support Staff

Instructions

1. Present the team-approved suggestion during the support-staff meeting.
2. Ensure that the suggestion is valid. A valid suggestion will improve safety, quality, delivery, or cost and be within the expense budget.
3. Decide whether to implement the suggestion.
4. Provide the team leader with an answer quickly. Choose a maximum target response time, such as two weeks. If a suggestion is rejected, explain the reason(s) for the rejection.
6. Create an action-item log.
7. Implement the suggestion as soon as possible. Choose a maximum target implementation time, such as two months.
8. Write the implementation date and number on the suggestion log.
9. Update the suggestion chart on the team board.
10. File the suggestion forms in chronological order.

Chapter 14: Workplace Organization

Creating the Image That Sets the Standards

An organization's image delivers a clear message about how a company operates. An organization's marketing literature goes through an elaborate process of graphic design and presentation to communicate standards of excellence. Similarly, a company's physical environment communicates its standards of excellence and performance.

Workplace organization defines the culture and work ethic of a company. It also defines the standards regarding how people function and present themselves. Contract workers and visitors will immediately recognize and adapt to these standards.

It is recommended that an organization implement the Five Basics of Workplace Organization prior to any process-improvement initiative. Successful implementation of the Five Basics of Workplace Organization will provide a boost in employee morale, highlight nonconformances, identify scrap-generating issues, lower inventory, and improve efficiency.

The Five Basics of Workplace Organization

Below is a rendition of workplace organization introduced as part of the Toyota Production System. The Five Basics of Workplace Organization are as follows:

Five Basics	Description
Cleanliness	Keep work area clean, spotless, or pure. Keep area clear of scrap and dirt. Maintain cleanliness of tools, fixtures, and equipment exterior. Remove items not related to the work activity. Designate an area for personal effects.
Orderliness	Keep work area orderly, organized, or methodical. Designate a place for tools and materials. Label and identify area of intended contents. Develop a process to communicate material replenishment or oversupply.
Tidiness	Keep work area neat and compact. Design the most practical and efficient work area. Lay out materials and scrap to flow into designated holding areas. Maintain the least

amount of material inventory in the work area. Move frequently used tools and materials closer to the point of use.

Process Define the areas of responsibility. List the expectations, and create a compliance checklist. Define the survey frequency, and conduct a baseline survey. Conduct training, and provide the tools and materials to accomplish the expectations. Conduct routine surveys.

Discipline Communicate the importance of process compliance to achieve performance standards. Develop a set of performance metrics for the entire company, for each department, and for each team. Integrate 5S as part of the performance-review process.

Implementation

A well-defined audit checklist establishes standards and dictates the level of success at implementing an effective workplace-organization campaign.

The five-step implementation process is as follows:

1. **Define areas of responsibilities**. Get a floor plan of your building or space, and divide the area for each team. Allocate common aisleways to teams so that the entire layout of the building is assigned to a specific team.

2. **Create a checklist of standards**. Create a simple audit checklist that defines expectations or standards. Performance should be measured by the number of compliant items on the checklist.

3. **Provide performance feedback**. Conduct routine (monthly) audits. Discuss the audit results with the team. Encourage the team to improve the score at least one point per month.

4. **Post the performance scorecard**. Create a simple scorecard showing the number of

compliant items in the checklist. Chart the progress monthly.

5. **Provide resources to implement workplace organization**. Provide the necessary tools and equipment required for the team to improve the 5S audit.

Workplace Organization

Manufacturing Five Basics Audit Checklist

Here is an example checklist for manufacturing.

Cleanliness

#	Item	Yes	No
1.	Area is free of scrap, litter, and dirt.		
2.	Irrelevant items are not stored in the area.		
3.	Trash and scrap containers are emptied before overflowing.		
4.	Postings are relevant and up to date.		
5.	Equipment exterior and paint finish appears clean.		
6.	Tools and fixtures are kept clean.		
7.	Floor marking appears clean and clearly defines the work area.		

Orderliness

#	Item	Yes	No
8.	Aisleways are clearly defined by floor tape or paint.		
9.	Aisleways and safety equipment are clear from any obstruction.		
10.	Materials, equipment, and fixtures have designated areas.		
11.	Designated areas clearly identify inspection and test status.		
12.	Designated areas are labeled to indicate their intended contents.		
13.	Items are maintained within the designated area.		
14.	Materials are not leaning against walls, pillars, or equipment.		
15.	The tool and fixture area is organized and labeled.		
16.	Personal items are consolidated in a designated area.		

Tidiness	**Yes**	**No**
17. Materials are stacked neatly, and postings are mounted squarely.		
18. Frequently used materials, tools, and fixtures are located close to the point of use.		
19. Materials, procedures, and tools are easily accessible.		

Process	**Yes**	**No**
20. Sufficient cleaning tools and supplies are provided to the work area.		
21. The storage area for cleaning tools and supplies is clean and organized.		
22. Procedures are written for routine cleaning and maintenance.		
23. The training log verifies training of team members.		

Discipline	**Yes**	**No**
24. The Five Basics review is conducted routinely.		
25. Scorecards or charts provide feedback to team members.		

Workplace Organization

Office Five Basics Audit Checklist

Below is an example checklist for the office environment.

Cleanliness	Yes	No
1. Area is free of scrap, litter, and dirt.		
2. Irrelevant items are not stored in the area.		
3. Trash and scrap containers are emptied before overflowing.		
4. Postings are relevant and up to date.		
5. Work stations and office equipment exteriors are clean.		
6. Materials are not stored behind furniture and storage cabinets.		

Orderliness	Yes	No
7. Office layout provides easy access to each workstation.		
8. Aisleways, circuit breakers, emergency exits, and other safety equipment are clear of any obstruction.		
9. Documents and materials have designated inbound, in-process, outbound, and storage locations.		
10 Nonconforming and sample materials are labeled.		
11. Binders, folders, and containers are labeled with their intended contents.		
12. Items are maintained within the designated area.		
13. Materials are not leaning against walls, pillars, or office equipment.		

14.	Power cords and cables are kept out of sight.		
15.	Business-use postings are limited to a designated area.		
16.	Personal effects are limited to a designated area.		

Tidiness		Yes	No
17.	Binders, folders, containers, and materials are neatly stored.		
18.	Postings are mounted squarely and appear organized.		
19.	Reminder notes are neat and tidy and do not dominate the work center.		

Process		Yes	No
20.	If a cleaning service is not provided, sufficient cleaning tools and supplies area provided to the work area.		
21.	The storage area for cleaning tools and supplies is clean and orderly.		

Discipline		Yes	No
22.	Guidelines are documented for maintaining a clean and organized work area.		
23.	The training log verifies training of team members.		
24.	The Five Basics review is conducted routinely.		
25.	A scorecard or chart provides feedback to team members.		

Workplace Organization

Step-by-Step Procedures
Workplace Organization

Workplace Organization

Assigning Areas of Responsibility

Instructions

1. Post a laminated map of the department in the support-staff meeting room.
2. Draw the department boundary with the support staff's help.
3. Split the department into areas of team responsibility. Label each team area on the map.
4. Conduct an initial Five Basics survey of each team area. The entire support staff should walk around for this initial survey.
5. Indicate each team's score on the map.
6. Chart the average score of all the teams on the support-staff board.
7. Set a realistic goal for the department's average Five Basics score.
8. Draw the goal with a black horizontal line.
9. Create action plans with each team to raise each team's score one or two points per month.
10. Insert time into the production schedule for cleaning and organizing the workplace. Use downtime, changeover, breaks, overtime, and so on.
11. Acquire cleaning supplies.

Conducting the Five Basics Survey

Instructions

1. Conduct the survey with the team leader and supervisor on a regular schedule each month.
2. Record the team name, team leader's name, surveyor name, and date at the top of a blank survey form.
3. Walk through the team area, discussing positive and negative changes since the last survey.
4. Mark each category as a yes if it has been taken care of or a no if improvement is still required.
5. Note items that are out of place in the Notes section. Note praise, concerns, or suggestions in the margins.
6. Count the number of yeses as the survey score.
7. Post the survey on the team board, over the previous month's.
8. Update the Workplace Organization chart on the team board.
9. Review the survey at the next team meeting.
10. Review the survey scores and department average at the next support-staff meeting.
11. Use the suggestion process to improve the area.

Workplace Organization

Chapter 15: Effective Job Performance Reviews

The Job Performance Rveiew (JPR) system is designed to be data driven and objective and requires minimal effort for the manager. It has been field tested and implemented in various-sized companies and industries.

Design Considerations

The following factors were considered in the development of the JPR system:

- The performance measures for each job position must support the department goals.
- Performance data must be quick and easy to access.
- Performance standards must be clearly defined.
- It should take the manager no more than five minutes to gather the data and complete a JPR.
- The JPR session should take no more than ten minutes.
- The JPR ratings should be easily linked to wage adjustments or compensation models.

Effective Job Performance Reviews

Rating System

Unlike traditional review systems, which use school-like grading systems, the JPR system uses a unique rating system. The starting point of the rating system is always at the Expected (5) level, and the data, being positive or negative, moves the rating to the set increments. The numerical ratings are provided in the chart below, and a description of each follows.

0	Change required
1 to 4	Contributing
5	Expected
6 to 9	Commendable
10	Exceptional

Change Required

The employee fails to deliver the expected performance. Performance-data documentation is required to support this rating. High levels of performance documentation are required. Performance reviews are given at a higher frequency, such as monthly or even weekly. Disciplinary action or even the warning process for termination is initiated.

Contributing

The employee performs below the standards of expectation. Performance-data documentation is required to support this rating. The manager may identify areas for improvement, begin the probationary process, or increase the review frequency.

Expected

The employee performs to standards or meets expected outcomes. This is the starting point of the rating scale. Use performance data to justify awarding a higher or lower rating. This is the only rating that does not require any performance documentation.

Commendable

The employee exceeds the expected levels of performance. Performance-data documentation is required to support this rating. He or she consistently goes beyond the performance standards on a month-to-month basis.

Exceptional

The employee consistently exceeds the established standards of performance on a year-to-year basis. This is a rare rating to award. Performance-data documentation is required to support this rating.

Components of a Job-Performance Review

Every JPR document will contain the following:

1. **List of performance measures**: A list of performance measures, the definition of each performance measure, and sources of data.

2. **Rating sheet:** A graduated scale of outcomes and the corresponding rating.

3. **Performance summary**: Rating of each performance item, noting the associated documentation to support the rating above and below the Expected (5) level.

Performance Measures

Performance measures are not limited to items that directly impact an individual. Total company, department, and team performance need to be considered.

Most performance measures are identified in the team meeting area. You can use some of the team performance measures and account for the individual impact of each item. Here is an example:

Defects Produced (1) Team
(2) Individual

If team performance measures are not available, use the planning matrix to identify potential items.

	Input (supplier)	Process (team)	Output (finished product)
Safety	Hazardous material leaks	Accidents and near misses	Stack height compliance
Quality	Defects received	Defects produced	Defects shipped
Delivery	On-time delivery	Schedule compliance	On-time delivery
Cost	Purchase-price variance	Productivity	Purchase-price variance
Continuous Improvement	NCR-CAR	NCR-CAR Suggestions 5S score	NCR-CAR

Each performance measure must be clearly defined and must identify the source(s) of the data.

Also consider process-compliance and process-improvement items. Managers and supervisors can collect observations and use them as performance data.

Not all performance data is collected by an ERP-MRP or computer system. The manager may have to develop a performance data-collection form. If this is the case, every effort should be made to keep the form easy to use and submit it on a routine basis.

Example Performance Measures

Department and Company Performance Measures

1. On-Time Delivery
Definition: Product delivery to customer on or before the due date

Source of data: Monthly service-level report

2. Productivity
Definition: Total units produced per labor hour

Source of data: Shop-floor management data

3. Customer Feedback
Definition: Performance feedback from customers

Source of data: Customer feedback and customer incident reports

Individual Performance Measures

4. Internal Defects
Definition: Defects reported by rewind or folder-gluer operations

Source of data: Scrap form completed by finishing department

5. Productivity

Definition: Total shift good footage produced per labor hour

Source of data: Shop-floor management data

6. Compliance to Policy and Procedure

Definition: Compliance with corporate and department policies, guidelines, directives, and procedures

Source of data: Exceptional and substandard performance documented by the supervisor or manager

Performance Standards

Standards of performance can be gathered based on historical data or a cascade from the department goal. Make sure the goals are attainable.

Rating Sheet

A graduated scale of performance outcomes lists the appropriate rating for each item. This will make it easy for the manager to provide an objective and consistent rating. Here is an example:

Item	Outcome	Rating
Nonconformance reports (NCRs)	Additional NCRs	−1 for each
	2 NCRs	5
	0 NCRs	+1 for every quarter

Effective Job Performance Reviews

Example JPR Rating Sheet

	Performance Standards	Value	Rating
1	On-time Delivery	100%	10
		99%	7
		98%	5
		97%	3
		96%	0

2	Department Productivity	2200	10
		1900	7
		1600	5
		1500	3
		1400	0

3	Customer Feedback	0	10
		5	7
		10	5
		15	3
		20	0

5	Internal Defects	3 Y with 0	10
		1 Y with 0	7
		3	5
		6	3
		9	0

6	Individual Productivity	See Machine Center Standards Sheet	10
			7
			5
			4 - 3
			0

7	Compliance with Policy & Procedure	++	10
		+	7
		0	5
		1 – 2 UO	4 - 3
		3 UO	0

Example Performance Summary

Name _____   JPR Review Period _____

	Rating	Weight	Score	Supporting Data
1. On-time Delivery		1		
2. Department Productivity		1		
3. Customer Feedback		1		
4. Internal Defects		1		
5. Individual Productivity		1		
6. Compliance with Policy & Procedure		1		
Sum of Column		8		
Overall JPR Rating				

Signatures

_____   _____   _____
Employee   Supervisor   HR Manager

Completing a JPR Form

Use the rating scale to reference the performance outcome and determine the JPR rating for each item. List supporting documents to justify a rating above or below the Expected (5) level. Write down any additional facts in the Notes section.

Calculate the total JPR rating for the period. Keep in mind that a rating of Expected (5) is a positive rating.

Review Process

Managers should realize that a JPR session is a historical review of performance data. The employee review should be scheduled for no more than ten minutes. Discussion regarding work issues or future job roles should be scheduled separately.

During the performance review, compare performance data with the set goals and objectives. In most cases, items that meet expectation (with a 5 rating) are discussed quickly. Items above and below the Expected (5) level will require a short discussion.

Linking JPR to Compensation

Translating an individual performance review into a numerical value provides the means for developing a compensation model for wage adjustments or bonuses.

In a wage-adjustment model, an organization develops a percentage distribution, as shown below:

Rating	Increase
7 and above	6%
6	5%
5	4%
4	3%
3 and below	0%

The distribution scale is applied to current employee wages in determining the total wage adjustments. The calculated total is compared to the budgeted amount, and the scale is adjusted up or down until the budgeted amount is matched.

Implementation

Implementation of a JPR system requires deliberate planning and execution. The implementation is a learning process for the entire company and requires patience from the supervisor and team members.

The implementation plan requires the supervisor and subordinates to develop the system jointly. This makes the JPR process transparent to the entire company and helps eliminate people's fear of JPRs.

Example Implementation Timetable

Week 1	Identify job positions
Week 2	Define performance measures
Week 3	Define rating worksheet
Week 4	Develop JPR documents
Week 5	Conduct employee overview
Weeks 6–8	Conduct first trial
Week 9	Review first trial
Weeks 9–12	Conduct second trial
Week 13	Review second trial
Weeks 14–17	Conduct third trial
Week 18	Review third trial
Week 19	Launch JPR systems

Step-by-Step Procedures
Effective Performance Review

JPR Implementation

Instructions

1. Define reporting relationships, referencing the organizational chart.
2. Define job positions.
3. Identify performance measures.
4. Define the source(s) of data.
5. Identify performance standards.
6. Develop a rating worksheet.
7. Develop the JPR form.
8. Conduct supervisor training.
9. Conduct employee training.
10. Conduct three monthly JPR trials.

JPR System Overview

Instructions

1. Conduct initial training.
2. Schedule start of review period.
3. Set up JPR filing system.
4. Document performance observations.
5. Complete JPR forms.
6. Submit JPR forms for review.
7. Update JPR forms.
8. Conduct individual reviews.
9. File JPR forms.

Completing a JPR Form

Instructions

1. Print JPR form.
2. Rate company and department JPR items.
3. Record company and department JPR items.
4. Copy a JPR form for each employee.
5. Rate individual JPR items.
6. Record individual items on JPR form.
7. Calculate total score.
8. Calculate overall JPR rating.
9. List supervisor notes.
10. Sign JPR forms.
11. Forward completed JPRs to HR or manager for validation.

Conclusion

Building a Citadel: A Strategic Guide to Lean

Over the years of training and helping organizations operate effectively and efficiently, I always assumed that each organization was unique and yet shared the same issues as most companies. A thorough situational analysis will enable you to adjust your approach to implementing and executing the fundamental processes outlined in this book.

Process improvement is an endless cycle of pursuing process excellence and adapting to changing markets and business environments. A structured organizational focus and process is the foundation at achieving process compliance, consistency, and predictability. It all starts with the strategic-management team outlining the organizational focus for achieving performance metrics.

The most rewarding aspect of my career as an educator and industrial engineer is witnessing people learn, apply the methods, win, and gain self-confidence. I do hope you find the same fulfilling experience as I did with the methods in this book.

Lean and Performance Driven

As an operations manager, I always remind myself and the management-support staff not to micromanage operations. Our primary role is to develop systems and procedures for the entire organization to be self-powered, self-driven, and self-correcting. Developing the fundamental structure described in this book requires patience and persistence.

Take one small step at a time, and effectively implement each step by validating the process with all the people impacted by the process. Engage everyone, and tell them that this is a new process for you and for all of them. Also, request their patience and feedback on how to make this process work successfully.

As you implement each chapter of this book, I hope you see incremental process improvements, enhanced performance outcomes, and improved employee morale. Soon after the fundamental structure is in place, I highly recommend that you explore the implementation of process-improvement tools used in initiatives such as Lean Six Sigma, Total Quality Management, and the Toyota Production System.

A

accounting systems · 49, 50
Arena of Competition · 21

B

Bath Record · 169
business enterprise optimization · 3
Business Process Mapping · 29, 41

C

Card System Design · 97
Common Goal · 109, 110, 120, 121
Compliance · 27, 111, 122, 131, 149, 162, 177, 179, 209, 212, 214, 215
Connector symbol · 36
Contingency · 17, 26
Continuous Improvement · 110, 111, 121, 122, 131, 149, 209
CorPlan · 16
Corporate Planning · 16
Corrective Action Plan · 84, 86
Corrective Action Process · 77, 78
Crystal Reports© · 5, 50, 51, 53

D

Dashboard · 63
Data Integrity · 27
Decision symbol · 35, 39
Diagnostic Measures · 45, 46
Diagnostics measures · 42

E

Enterprise Resource Planning · 7, 49
Environmental Analysis · 23
ERP · 49, 50, 51, 89
Example Procedure Format · 174

H

Hawthorne Effect · 65

I

Input-Process-Output · 110, 111, 121, 122

K

Kaizen · 5, 65, 66, 67, 68, 69, 70, 71, 72, 74
Kaizen Blitz · 5
Kaizen Events · 5, 66
Kanban · 6, 87, 88, 89, 90, 91, 93, 94, 95, 96, 99, 100, 101, 166
Key Points · 32, 39, 40

L

Lean · 2, 5, 15
Line Connector · 33, 35

Manager's Guide to Lean and Performance

M

Main Steps · 32, 39
Management Review · 43, 44
Market Opportunities & Threats · 24
Meeting Agenda · 138, 155
Meeting Area · 133, 154
Microsoft© Project · i, 5, 55
Milestones · 55, 57
Mission Statement · 19
MRP · 49, 89

N

non-conformance · 6, 77, 78, 79, 80, 81, 82, 86
Non-Conformances · 106, 143

O

Objective · 17, 24, 69
ODBC connection · 52
Organization Strengths & Limitations · 21
Organizational discipline · 4, 7

P

PDCA · 5, 65, 69, 71, 72, 73, 74, 75
performance data · 105, 109, 120, 134, 141, 210, 216
Performance Data · 132, 134, 143, 179
Performance Feedback · 111, 123
Performance Goals · 136
performance measures · 110, 111, 121, 122, 123, 131, 143, 149, 150, 155, 156, 205, 208, 209, 218, 220
Performance Metrics · 4, 41, 42, 43, 44, 45, 46, 47, 107
Predecessor Tasks · 60
Process Compliance · 119, 159, 210
Process Flow · 30, 31, 33, 36
Process symbol · 34, 35, 36
Product-Service History Record · 169
Product-Service Master Record · 169
Program · 17
project management · 5, 55

Q

Quality Systems · i, 43, 45, 47

R

Regulatory Affairs · 43, 45, 47
Resource Assessment · 20
Root Cause · 83

S

Safety · 39, 43, 45, 47, 97, 98, 101, 110, 111
Scoreboard · 180
strategic plan · 4, 7, 15, 41
Strategic Plan · 15, 16, 17, 24, 26, 27, 41, 42
Strategic Planning · i, 3, 15, 16, 17, 27
Strategy · 16, 17, 25
Suggestions · 106, 111, 122, 131, 136, 143, 149, 152, 209

Index

Supplier Management · 166
Support Staff · 69, 103, 105, 106, 107, 115, 127, 141, 142, 143, 144, 148, 149, 156, 180, 182, 187, 190
Support Structure · 141
System · 172, 181, 182, 192, 206, 221

T

tasks · 56, 57, 60, 61, 109, 113
Team and Management Support structure · 142
Team Leader · 112, 113, 114, 115, 124, 125, 126, 127, 132, 148
Team Representative · 112, 113, 124
Team Structure · 130
Teamwork · 109, 120

Terminator · 33
Total Quality Management · 15
training matrix · 172, 175, 177, 178
Training Matrix · 163
Training Method · 40
Two-bin System · 94

U

Undesired Processes · 38

W

Work Instructions · 30
Work Teams · 117
Workplace Organization · i, 136, 152, 191, 192, 201, 203

Made in the USA
Middletown, DE
25 July 2015